The Consulting Room and Beyond

Psychoanalysis in a New Key L
Volume 9

Donnel B. Stern
Series Editor

When music is played in a new key, the melody does not change, but the notes that make up the composition do: change in the context of continuity, continuity that perseveres through change. "Psychoanalysis in a New Key" publishes books that share the aims psychoanalysts have always had, but that approach them differently. The books in the series are not expected to advance any particular theoretical agenda, although to this date most have been written by analysts from the Interpersonal and Relational orientations.

The most important contribution of a psychoanalytic book is the communication of something that nudges the reader's grasp of clinical theory and practice in an unexpected direction. "Psychoanalysis in a New Key" creates a deliberate focus on innovative and unsettling clinical thinking. Because that kind of thinking is encouraged by exploration of the sometimes surprising contributions to psychoanalysis of ideas and findings from other fields, "Psychoanalysis in a New Key" particularly encourages interdisciplinary studies. Books in the series have married psychoanalysis with dissociation, trauma theory, sociology, and criminology. The series is open to the consideration of studies examining the relationship between psychoanalysis and any other field—for instance, biology, literary and art criticism, philosophy, systems theory, anthropology, and political theory.

But innovation also takes place within the boundaries of psychoanalysis, and "Psychoanalysis in a New Key" therefore also presents work that reformulates thought and practice without leaving the precincts of the field. Books in the series focus, for example, on the significance of personal values in psychoanalytic practice, on the complex interrelationship between the analyst's clinical work and personal life, on the consequences for the clinical situation when patient and analyst are from different cultures, and on the need for psychoanalysts to accept the degree to which they knowingly satisfy their own wishes during treatment hours, often to the patient's detriment.

The Consulting Room and Beyond

Psychoanalytic Work and Its Reverberations
in the Analyst's Life

THERESE RAGEN

Foreword by Donnel Stern

Routledge
Taylor & Francis Group
New York   London

Routledge
Taylor & Francis Group
270 Madison Avenue
New York, NY 10016

Routledge
Taylor & Francis Group
27 Church Road
Hove, East Sussex BN3 2FA

© 2009 by Taylor & Francis Group, LLC

Printed in the United States of America on acid-free paper
10 9 8 7 6 5 4 3 2 1

International Standard Book Number-13: 978-0-88163-472-3 (Softcover) 978-0-88163-471-6 (Hardcover)

Library of Congress Cataloging-in-Publication Data

Ragen, Therese.
    The consulting room and beyond : psychoanalytic work and its reverberations in the
analyst's life / Therese Ragen.
        p. ; cm. -- (Psychoanalysis in a new key book series ; v. 9)
    Includes bibliographical references and index.
    ISBN 978-0-88163-471-6 (hardcover : alk. paper) -- ISBN 978-0-88163-472-3
    (softcover : alk. paper)
    1. Psychoanalysis. 2. Psychotherapist and patient. I. Title. II. Series.
    [DNLM: 1. Psychoanalytic Therapy. 2. Professional-Patient Relations. 3.
Psychotherapeutic Processes. WM 460.6 R141c 2008]

    RC506.R336 2008
    616.89'17--dc22   2008017752

Visit the Taylor & Francis Web site at
http://www.taylorandfrancis.com

and the Routledge Web site at
http://www.routledgementalhealth.com

CONTENTS

Foreword

You have never read anything like the essays in this book. Quite simply, Therese Ragen has invented a new form of psychoanalytic writing. I read the first of these essays when I was the editor of *Contemporary Psychoanalysis*. I thought they were remarkable, and we published them. The pieces that Dr. Ragen has written since then are even better.

The category that comes closest to encompassing this work within its boundaries is the personal essay. A personal essay addresses a particular topic but, unlike the traditional essay, makes no pretense of objectivity. The point is not the revelation, via the writer's analysis, of something new about the subject of the essay—or at least the point is not only such revelation. The personal essay accomplishes something in that vein, but by addressing what the topic of the essay means to the author. We read the personal essay, therefore, not only to learn but also to experience something along with the writer, and that something generally has considerable personal significance in the writer's world.

All of this is certainly true of Dr. Ragen's work, which is not only personal but also often deeply moving. One of the two primary subjects Dr. Ragen addresses is the place of her work as a psychoanalyst in the broader bounds of her life. We learn about what it is like for her to be a psychoanalyst. What are the joys, fears, hopes, and dreads that her work contributes to her life? What is her work like for her when she is out of the office? Who are her patients to her, not only in the office but also at night and on the weekends? What part do they play in events of her life that, on the face of it, have nothing to do with them? (We all know that such events outside the office do come to evoke feelings and flashes of thought about patients—this is part of Dr. Ragen's message.) These are not questions that psychoanalysts have written very much about, although of course every single analyst experiences, every day, some version of an answer to them. For this reason alone, these essays will be gripping for psychoanalysts. Actually, this may also be a good reason for the appeal these essays may very well have for interested laypeople. It is rare that an analyst has written about what it is like to be someone who does this work, and no one has written about that subject with this degree of candor and subtlety. Dr. Ragen's respectful and deeply felt accounts will certainly relieve any laypeople who have worried that they disappear from the analyst's mind when the office door closes behind them.

But the place of her work in her life is only half of what Dr. Ragen writes about. The other half is the place of her *life* in her *work*. This is an equally fascinating angle on the relationship between psychoanalysis and living. The object of Dr. Ragen's interest, when she is taking this perspective, far exceeds countertransference. Dr. Ragen tells us about the continuous impact of the events of her existence—and her reactions to them, large and small—and on her work with her patients.

An introduction to Dr. Ragen's work would be incomplete without mention of its narrative drive. These pieces do not read like essays, more like short stories. You will find yourself more than once tempted to turn to the end of one of them to find out what happens. Other writers have worked this vein (Harold Lindner and Irwin Yalom come to mind). But Dr. Ragen's "stories" are compulsively readable, yet without sacrificing an iota of clinical sophistication. All psychoanalysts will recognize every nuance of what she writes.

To this point, my description of these essays would not necessarily be inconsistent with the definition of the personal essay. But Dr. Ragen goes a step further than I have yet described. She brings all of this experience—the impact of her life on her work, and her work on her life—into relation with psychoanalytic ideas. Dr. Ragen is not only a talented memoirist (we have too few memoirs about work, in any field) but also a sophisticated psychoanalytic thinker. She somehow manages to bring her experience of her work and her life to bear on questions that further our understanding of dissociation and other matters that are usually addressed only in traditional scholarly essays. This is a notable accomplishment, made that much more notable by Dr. Ragen's avoidance of sentimentality in conveying great depth of feeling, and of intellectualization in conveying how these affect-laden events illuminate theory.

We could say that what Dr. Ragen is doing is simultaneously contextualizing her life in her work and her work in her life, and contextualizing all of it in psychoanalytic thought. This is a neat enough formulation, but it is just as seriously imperfect a description of the essays you are about to read as it is of clinical work itself. In clinical practice, the patient's experience is contextualized by the analyst's, and the analyst's by the patient's; and for the analyst, the whole is also contextualized in the history and literature of the field. But as useful as it often is to think this way, it is a hopelessly inadequate invocation of the totality of relatedness, as any description must be. Relatedness is more truly seamless than it is any combination of entities. It is unto itself. As are the essays you are about to read.

Donnel B. Stern

Acknowledgments

How do I thank Molly Daniels, with whom I discovered my love of writing in her Clothesline School of Writing classes during the 1990s? She believed in me as a writer before I believed in myself. I am forever grateful to my friend and colleague Kathy Kearney, who, as my "first reader," read and encouraged me through draft upon draft of the chapters in this book over the years I have worked on it. My deep thanks to my friend and colleague Debra Gold, who thoughtfully and incisively gave me feedback on the "almost final" drafts of each chapter. The support and enthusiasm of my friends Maureen Cassidy, Noreen Jordan, Sheila Linehan, and Betty Smith meant so much to me over the course of this project.

On Fridays for the past 8 years, I have met in a psychoanalytic consultation group with Philip Bromberg, Debbie Birnbaum, Melinda Gellman, and Alan Kintzer. We have been companions into the joy and pain of the depths of each others' clinical work, including portions of this book, and I thank them. Thank you to Donnel Stern, who as editor of the journal *Contemporary Psychoanalysis* and then as editor of this book series, understood and appreciated what I was attempting to do in my writing.

At a 2001 conference on the anxiety of authorship and women writing in psychoanalysis, I heard Carole Maso (2000) give a reading from her book *Break Every Rule: Essays on Language, Longing and Desire.* Out of that grew a writing group of eight women psychoanalysts, which has been meeting monthly and for a summer retreat each year with Carole. I thank them all—Anna Bella Bushra, Liz Goren, Anita Herron, Linda Luz-Alterman, Jill Salberg, Melanie Suchet, and Alexandra Woods. The reflective and respectful way in which we hold each others' work has nurtured and sustained my writing self over the past 6 years. A powerful and steadying presence, Carole has called forth the best in me. And, thank you to Margaret Little (1985, 1987), whom I first admired in graduate school for her awe-inspiring account of her own psychoanalysis with D. W. Winnicott, and Sándor Ferenczi for the very personal *Clinical Diary* (1932/1988) he left us.

Lastly, I want to thank my patients, both those I've written about in this book and those I haven't, for allowing me to walk with them on their courageous life journeys.

1 Legacy*

When a patient of mine and his twin brother were a little over a
year old, his brother died in his crib in the middle of their nap
one afternoon. My patient had often climbed out of his crib and into
his brother's. That afternoon when their mother came to get them up,
my patient was in his brother's crib and his brother lay next to him
no longer breathing. The cause of death was determined to be sudden
infant death syndrome, but my patient often wondered if he might have
somehow killed his brother, maybe suffocating him with a pillow or a
blanket. He had no memory of his brother dying, and it disturbed him
that he could not remember not having killed him. He wanted to be sure
he had nothing to do with his brother dying.

I talked about this in our Friday consultation group, which consists
of Debbie Birnbaum, Melinda Gellman, Alan Kintzer, and me meeting
with Philip Bromberg, a senior analyst from New York University, to
discuss our work. As we talked about my patient and his brother, I had
a growing sense of urgency inside and asked Phil, "Do you think he
could have killed him?"

I have no recollection of what Phil said, but shortly after that I began
to not really follow him or understand what he was saying. I heard the
words, but just felt, "Huh?" Phil stopped talking and looked at me and

*An earlier version of this chapter appeared in the *Texas Review*, 23(3/4), 2004.

asked, "Are you all right?" I told him I felt shook up inside, that something was wrong, but I didn't know what and asked him why he asked, like he knew something I didn't, he knew I wasn't all right, in a clearer way than I did. Then we had to end, and it got worse. As I walked home my brain felt like it was fragmenting, a physical feeling of fragmenting. It scared me. I'd never felt that way before. I started to feel like I wasn't connected to myself, a strange and unfamiliar feeling.

The next week Phil asked again when I walked in if I had been okay and said he almost called me to make sure afterwards. I described how I'd felt while walking home afterwards and how it had gone away and I had no idea what it was about. It didn't seem to fit at all with what we had been talking about. I ended by saying, "It will probably come up again." I think Phil said, "I'm sure it will."

* * *

One month later, I was in a New York State courtroom having been called for jury duty. The two men at the defendant's table began sizing us up as we walked into the courtroom. The accused man's eyes darted from prospective juror to prospective juror. His attorney scrutinized us slowly, one by one. When the judge read the indictment, she said the defendant, Juan, was accused of murder and my hands started to tremble slightly, the way they do sometimes when I am anxious.

The district attorney talked to the first group of 16 who'd been called into the jurors' box for questioning. He stood directly in front of me just a few feet from the front row where I was sitting. He was telling us about the case. He said that everyone involved in it was a self-admitted drug dealer—the defendant, the victim, the witnesses. That's how they made their living—selling drugs. And that had been the apparent reason for the murder. The man who'd been murdered hadn't paid drug money he owed the murderer. The district attorney said this was going to be a gruesome case and a graphic case. He said the jurors would see bloody photographs of the murdered man who was gunned down in his car, shot three times in the head.

* * *

It was 1946 when my mother and father, a few days away from their first wedding anniversary, came down the steps of a train from St. Petersburg, Florida, to the Englewood train station on the South side of Chicago. In her arms, Mom carried Bill, my oldest brother, then just 4 months old, and Dad had their carry-on luggage. They were returning from vacation at my mother's family's home in St. Petersburg. When they got to the bottom of the stairs my mother's uncle, John Carey, was waiting for them. He told them Grandpa, Dad's father, had been shot by the Mafia.

Grandpa had worked for years as the circulation manager of the *Chicago Herald Examiner*, and then started and owned Continental Wire Service and the *Green Sheet*, the daily racing news form. After some time, the Mafia wanted to take over my grandfather's business but Grandpa said no.

They told him they'd kill him if he didn't turn over the business to them. But Grandpa dug in and refused to let the Mafia have it. Driving to work one morning, he noticed a car parked across the street from their house follow him. He sped up, and the other car did also. Grandpa was only a few blocks from the Gresham police station and sped the rest of the way there. The other car continued on.

Even then, Grandpa refused to comply with the Mob's demand. Friends had tried to talk Grandpa into going back to the family's Miami Beach home for the spring, thinking things might blow over. Grandpa responded there was only one way he was going to leave Chicago and that was if it was "God's will."

My parents were living with my maternal grandmother not far from the Ragens' home. My mom remembers after the shooting that each morning a Chicago police car waited outside her mother's home to escort my father to Michael Reese Hospital, where Grandpa was in critical condition.

* * *

When the district attorney in the courtroom said the jurors would see the photographs of the murdered man in his car, I immediately saw an image in my mind of my grandfather driving home from work one day and approaching the intersection of 35th and State. A car was stalled in the middle of the intersection, blocking traffic. I saw a look of fear pass across Grandpa's face, thinking it's a setup. His mind went to how to get out of the thin line of cars to make a U-turn and go home another way. After the chase to the Gresham police station, Grandpa got a body-guard. The man usually drove in a separate car behind Grandpa, but that day he had called in sick, so Grandpa was driving his own car and the man who was usually Grandpa's driver was acting as his bodyguard and driving in the car behind him. I saw Grandpa check in his rearview mirror and roll down the window to signal to the driver he was going to make a U-turn. Grandpa saw the anxiety in the driver's face, and just then a truck pulled up beside him. The tarp on it went up, and three men with submachine guns came out from underneath it, blasting bullets into Grandpa's car.

Grandpa was rushed to Michael Reese Hospital with multiple gunshot wounds, and, somehow, he lived. They performed surgery, and Grandpa was put in a single room near intensive care under the watch of two Chicago policemen, one at his door and one at the end of the hallway.

My uncle James, my dad's oldest brother, worked with my grandfather running Continental Wire and the *Green Sheet*. He flew out on a service flight to Paris the day after Grandpa was shot and never returned to the United States.

Over the next several weeks, Grandpa began recuperating. He was doing well initially, but then died of kidney failure, secondary to the gunshot wounds he had suffered.

It was only when the woman next to me offered me a Kleenex that I realized I was crying and could not stop.

* * *

The next morning I sat in Starbucks at 78th and Lex reading over my notes from a session with a patient in preparation for the Friday consultation group with Alan, Debbie, Melinda, and Phil. I was going to present that day and sat at a small round table reading and rereading my scribbled handwriting on the yellow legal paper in front of me. At one point my mind floated off—or something floated into my mind—about being in court, about the district attorney standing in front of the jury box saying the jurors would have to look at graphic photographs of the dead man in the car. I caught myself drifting off thinking about that and realized how I was pushing myself to do what I needed to do, to get ready for the consultation, to reread my notes, but there was this other reality from the courtroom sitting right underneath that one, pressing up on me.

I sat in Starbucks mesmerized and found myself in a reverie about that day in the consultation group when I felt so shook up without understanding why. My eyes fixed on but I wasn't really seeing the young woman at the table across from me. She was hunched over her book in her heavy blue winter coat, seemingly oblivious to the world. But she wasn't oblivious to my stare. I suddenly became aware she was looking at me, had felt me staring through her and was uncomfortable. It jarred me out of my reverie, and in coming out of it I realized what had happened to me that day in Phil's office. We'd begun to touch on another reality in me—a reality of terror and murder buried inside of me.

I left Starbucks and went to the group and told them what had just happened, how now I knew what had happened to me in the group that day 3 months before. And I told them the story of what happened to me in court, how feelings about and images of my grandfather dying flooded me and how disconcerting it was to me.

* * *

Melinda said, "Our whole professional life is geared towards using our feelings, being open to our feelings as a way of understanding other people. When we're put in a room with violent people, of course we're going to feel frightened."

I told her I kept thinking, "What's wrong with me? No one normal would be feeling what I was feeling and crying like I was crying."

"Maybe we should all be sitting in those courtrooms crying. Maybe that's what would really be normal," Melinda said.

"I just don't have any ego strength or something. It's embarrassing," I said.

She said, "You wouldn't be saying that if you were listening to a patient tell you what you're telling me. You'd be thinking about transgenerational trauma, that's what you're talking about experiencing, the transmission of trauma from one generation to the next."

"But I didn't even know my grandfather," I said. "He was killed 4 years before I was even born."

"It doesn't matter," she said. "It's inside of you."

Phil said to me, "You sound like every other person reliving unprocessed trauma—terrified and ashamed."

"Unprocessed trauma?" I said.

"Yes. It's the nature of trauma that it's extremely difficult to process. It's so out of the ordinary. It's so out of the realm of common experience, your day-to-day experience of your self. It overwhelms you. You can't digest it. It's as though you have nowhere to put it in what has been your experience of life and of yourself up to that point, so you encapsulate it and kind of put it off to the side of the core of yourself, and there it exists, like a self without a voice. The feelings only come to feel they are a real part of your self when you talk about them and they come alive emotionally in the mind of another. If your feelings go unrecognized, you have to hold onto them as though they don't exist. And then something happens later on, like your experience in court, that triggers the trauma, and it all comes back, flooding you with the walled-off feelings, the shame and terror. It's as if you're back in the original trauma, and, in fact, part of you is. You're not remembering the event. You're reliving it in the here and now as a real event with all the feeling of that real event. That's what happened to you in court: Your grandfather's murder, the actual event of it and all that followed, has lived inside you in a part of your self that you were thrust into in that courtroom the other day."

"But why do I feel ashamed?"

"Because you feel like you're going to be overwhelmed. You feel weak and needy. And you want to talk about what is happening to you. You need to talk about it, but there's no one there to listen."

That night I talked on the phone to my sister Anne. I told her what happened, how I couldn't stop crying, how I kept thinking about Grandpa, and how I thought it wasn't normal and no one else in the family would have reacted that way. She said, "If I heard that lawyer say I'd have to look at graphic photographs of a man shot up in a car, I would have reacted exactly like you did." And then she told me she had softly cried all through the movie *The Godfather* when she saw it years ago.

A couple of nights later, I called my mother. As I picked up the phone, I thought of the old photograph someone had found among their family's pictures and sent to my mother just a year or so ago. It's a photograph someone had taken, for what reason no one knows, outside the church at Grandpa's funeral. It's a big black-and-white glossy photograph, probably 8″ by 10″. The family has just come down the stairs in front of the church and is walking toward the black limousines to take them to the cemetery. My father must have just passed the lens of the camera with his mother and youngest sister. All the men are in dark suits, and the women are all wearing black dresses and gloves and hats. My mother is wearing long black gloves up to her elbows and a pillbox hat with light netting that comes down over her face. Her face is so sad. It's filled with sadness. When I first looked at the photograph, I just sat and stared at my mother's face, surprised and perplexed and sad that she was sad. It wasn't her father who had died. I didn't know why she was sad. I sat and looked at it for a long time, trying to understand.

My mother knew I had been called for jury duty, and shortly into our phone call she asked me how it had gone. I wasn't sure how she'd respond, if she'd understand at all what I was going through, but I went ahead and told her. I told her the whole story and how upset I was and surprised that I got so upset, and then I asked her if she could understand it, if it made sense to her. She said, "Yes. You were probably feeling afraid being in the courtroom with an accused murderer, and then when they said the man was shot in his car it made you think of Grandpa and brought up the whole thing with Grandpa for you." She understood. But it wasn't only that she understood. It was that I could hear her listening. As I was telling her the story of what happened, I could hear her listening. I had been afraid she would cut me short or change the subject, but instead what I heard was the sound of my mother listening to every word I said.

* * *

Captive City (Demaris, 1969), a book about the Mafia in Chicago in the 1940s, quotes a Chicago police commander from that time saying that if Grandpa's murder was solved, half the Chicago Police Department would have jumped out of windows. The *Chicago Herald Examiner* reported that Grandpa had put incriminating information about the men who wanted his business in a safe deposit box that was to be given to the attorney general of Illinois in the event of his death. The paper also quoted Grandpa as saying if he was murdered, his sons would take over the business.

Most of what I know about Grandpa's murder, I discovered in college at the Chicago Public Library downtown and in some books that were written about the Chicago Mafia. My mother told me about it shortly after I began college. I was hungry to know more, but my mother didn't know the answers to many of my questions. When I asked her what Dad said to her when he came home after a day in court, she said, "He never spoke about it." It was after that that I went to the library over semester break and began to research more of the details of what had happened.

I never knew how to feel about what happened to Grandpa. It felt like there was some way I should feel about it, a way one *would* feel about it, but I didn't know what that way was. It felt confusing not to know what I should feel. It was as though if I knew what I should feel, then I'd know what I did feel. But it never got straightened out for me.

A few weeks after I got back to school from semester break, we were looking at the idea of legacy in a writing class I was taking. The professor read Dylan Thomas' "Do Not Go Gentle Into That Good Night" (1938). We were to listen and then write freely. I wrote,

Do not go gentle into the night.
Rage. Rage.

Do not go Grandpa. Stay with us. Bring us your warmth, your laughter. Show us your twinkling eyes. Don't go. We want to know you. Stay to be with us. You'll sweep us up on your knee. Our dad will smile again. His darkness will pass. Don't let them kill you. Stay with us. Give them what they want. Take your money and go. Your courage will not be your legacy to us. Your self-defeating mule headedness will be your legacy. Fear and anger is what we will be left with. Let them have what they want, Grandpa. Give them your business. But then we'd be ashamed of you and your legacy would be for us to feel weak and puny and humiliated. Die Grandpa, die. It's the right thing to do.

* * *

It wouldn't have been wrong for Grandpa to live. What was wrong was reality. There have been a few books written over the years that mention Grandpa's murder. One is *Captive City* (Demaris, 1969). Another is *Hoover: The Man and the Secrets* (Gentry, 1991), a biography of J. Edgar Hoover. According to *Hoover*, Grandpa went to see Hoover a month before he was shot. He told Hoover the incriminating information he'd put in the safe deposit box and asked Hoover for protection. Hoover said no, and one month later Grandpa was gunned down. *Captive City* says there were three witnesses to Grandpa's death.

When it came time for the trial, one had been murdered, one had moved to Texas, and the other had decided he hadn't seen anything.

When *Captive City* came out, I was in college. The book had a glossary in the back with brief bios of the Mafia men mentioned in the book and their addresses. It named the men who shot Grandpa. I was outraged they were alive and free and nothing had happened to them. I wanted to go to their houses and ring their front door-bells and stand there and say, "You killed my grandfather!" when they opened the door. I imagined them standing in the doorway with their heads hanging, speechless, feeling ashamed, mortified. I told my mother and she said, "Don't ever, ever do that. Don't even think about doing that."

I was watching the news one night in the early 1990s when I lived in Chicago. A story came on that one of the men who shot Grandpa, and who had been convicted of a crime he committed years after Grandpa was killed, when the Mafia's power was waning, was a sick, old man in jail and had appealed to the court to be lenient and to let him out. The story ran for several days. I don't know what happened to him, but I wanted to call the judge and urge him to never let that man out.

Each night that week after being in court, when I got home I read parts of Judith Herman's book *Trauma and Recovery* (1992). She talks about how important it is for people to reconstruct the story of their trauma in detail both factually and emotionally, living the feelings of the trauma in the telling of it. She says in reconstructing the story the trauma undergoes a transformation, becoming more vivid and real as well as felt to be more part of the self. It comes to be integrated more as a memory than a past that's buried alive.

One night that week I opened the Hoover book, *Hoover: The Man and the Secrets* (Gentry, 1991), before I left my office. It had a couple of pages about Grandpa's murder in it. I hadn't remembered some of what it said. I hadn't remembered that the author said Grandpa thought that whether he sold out to the Mafia or not, they would "eliminate" him, and I didn't know if the author really knew what he was talking about. I hadn't remembered a purported quote by Grandpa saying that he knew if he didn't sell out to them, "I'm putting a big X across my name." I had forgotten that it was Al Capone's branch of the Mafia, one of his "lieutenants," who ordered the hit. I didn't recall the book said that Hoover had guaranteed Grandpa protection before he was interviewed by the FBI, then when they finished interviewing him Hoover went back on his word, and someone—probably from the Justice Department, the author said—let the Mafia know Grandpa had "blabbed to the Feds," and he was shot a month later. And I didn't remember that the men who killed Grandpa had been associates in the Chicago Mob with Jack Ruby, the man who shot and killed Lee Harvey Oswald. Actually, I didn't remember most of what I'd read when that book came out 10 years ago.

* * *

That night I woke up from a dream. I was jogging down a street with an old friend, Betty Smith. She was running ahead of me. We talked as we ran. It was pitch black, and I couldn't see her but I could hear her. As we passed a house set back off the road, I heard the sound of threatening, menacing voices on the side of the road and could just barely see the dim figures of a small group of men standing there. A few seconds later, Betty screamed out for help. I ran to catch up to her. I still couldn't see her because it was so dark, but I could hear the sound of her footsteps running and her screams for help. Then all of a sudden, everything was quiet. She wasn't calling out, and there was no sound of her footsteps. It was silent and black. I ran to call the police and woke myself up screaming, "Help!"

* * *

I've often wondered how Grandpa's murder affected my father. Dad had a playful, zestful side to him and a wry sense of humor, but he was often in a dark and stormy state from which he would lash out with a biting temper. When my youngest brother, Tom, was about to graduate from college and leave home, my father slid into a deep depression, overcome I think by feelings he had struggled with for years. I wonder how much of the anguish he lived in was the result of his father's murder. He and his brothers didn't keep the family business. One day, I asked my mother what had happened to the safe deposit box that was to go to the attorney general. She told me, "Your father said, 'This is the end of it,'" and over his sisters' objections went to the bank, opened the safe deposit box, and tore up the papers. They sold the *Green Sheet* and Continental Wire Service to someone who had worked for Grandpa.

Did my dad feel disloyal to his father in destroying the incriminating information? Did he feel guilty he didn't take over the business? How afraid for his own and other family members', including my mother and brother's, lives had he been? And what of the impotent rage he must have felt from being unable to stop the Mafia from killing Grandpa and knowing who it was who killed him and that they would never be brought to justice? He wanted to leave the South side of Chicago, but stayed in deference to my mother's wish to be close by her mother and with the understanding that after Nana died they would move. Some 20 years later Nana died, and within the year my parents moved to the far North suburbs.

How much did Dad's fears about the safety of all of us derive from the fact of Grandpa's murder? Growing up, he instructed us to sit in the front pews on the side of St. Barnabas Church near the door so we could get out in case of fire. As we got older and went to the movies with our friends, he told us to get seats by an exit sign. A spotlight shone in our backyard at night, and the keys for the double locks were hung high up on the frames of the doors so that if people were burglarizing the house, they would be unable to assure themselves a quick exit and be discouraged from staying in the house. When my sisters Mary and Anne and I got older and moved upstairs to the renovated third floor, my father had the carpenter make a trap door in the floor above my brothers Bill and Joe's bedroom closet, with a ladder built into the closet to climb in case of fire. One Sunday morning I left a pan of bacon I was frying to tie my youngest brother Tom's shoes for Mass and a grease fire started, scorching the kitchen cabinets above the stove. After that my father had fire extinguishers installed on every floor of the house. When one of us took out the car as teenagers, Dad's parting words were always, "Lock the doors."

There are many moments I look back at and wonder whether they were influenced by Dad's reactions to Grandpa's murder. I remember being at weekday Mass with Dad at St. Barnabas. We sat and knelt and stood next to each other and recited the Latin responses aloud together. I felt peace and love at these times and felt like my father did too. When we were growing up we had a magnetic medallion of St. Christopher, the patron saint of travelers, affixed to the dashboard of the station wagon. I remember the special crucifix for Extreme Unction that hung in Mom and Dad's bedroom. Dad frequently took walks. When he was happy, he'd often walk along making big wide swings and clapping his hands. When he was down or angry, he'd walk with his head down. When he walked at night, he usually took a golf club with him to scare off any dogs that might approach.

Dad and my uncle Phil joined the Moose Lodge when we were little so that if either of them died, their families could go live at the Moose Lodge. I always felt guilty because there were moments I hoped he'd die so we could go live at the lodge. I imagined it being like a year-round sleep-away camp. As an adult I told my dad, and he laughed and thought it was funny.

Dad became furious when a fly got into the house. He would yell, "Who let the fly into the house?" then try to trap it in a room, closing all the doors behind it, and kill it. His mood was sour afterwards. One day at the pool the diving coach said it was time for me to start doing my dives off the high board. I couldn't get the one-and-a-half flip down, and it stung horribly when I hit the water wrong. I went home very upset and told my parents what had happened. My father became furious and was going to get in the car right then and drive over to the pool to confront the diving coach. My mother insisted that he not do that, and it took her a while to calm him down enough that he didn't go.

* * *

Auerhahn and Laub (1984) categorized trauma into two kinds—trauma through events and trauma in which other persons deliberately attempt to destroy an individual (e.g., through war, murder, or torture). In those instances in which other persons deliberately attempt to destroy an individual, what is also destroyed is the victim's expectation of the basic safety and security within human relationships. The everyday illusions of benign interpersonal relatedness are shattered, leaving the individual feeling vulnerable and lonely, no longer at home in the world.

In an article about traumatic memory and the intergenerational transmission of the Holocaust, Anne Adelman (1995) conjectured that the ultimate obstacle to a parent telling one of his or her own children about the experience is that parent and child "jointly defend against intense despair and grief, fearing that if the floodgates were to open, they would both be swept away in the torrent" (p. 355).

Adelman (1995) further noted that many parents who have suffered trauma are "deeply ambivalent about what and how much to tell their children directly about their traumatic experiences" (p. 360). Fresco (1984) spoke of the deeply held desire on the parents' part to spare their children the burden of knowing the suffering they themselves had undergone. For the next generation, however, narrating the legacy of the trauma often serves "as a way to integrate and transcend the trauma."

Ghislaine Boulanger (2002a, 2002b), who has written on adult onset trauma talks of various kinds, talked about the experience of being traumatized as an adult as one that leaves the individual in a state of ongoing dread. She said,

> When indifferent reality cannot be assimilated or altered psychically, when it cannot be symbolized, it becomes traumatic reality. It is a reality that sticks in the psychic craw and cannot be dislodged. The survivor is always choking on the fact of it, always fearing a repetition of the breakdown that has already happened. (Winnicott, 1974, Boulanger, 2002a, p. 36)

Adult onset trauma "shakes the very foundation of a formerly solid core self" (Boulanger, 2002b, p. 68).

Children of survivors of trauma span the continuum from wanting to know nothing about what happened to their parent(s) to wanting to know it all. Frequently there is "an overpowering need of the first generation to bury the ashes of the past" (Prince, 1985, p. 37), which limits how much they are willing to communicate with their children about it.

On the children's part, the wish for knowledge is for some their way of putting the past behind and going on less fettered by conscious and unconscious fears and dreads. A search for identification with the parent, a way of knowing their parent and coming to feel close to him or her, motivates some children's desire for knowledge. What is involved for some are wishes to restore the parent's unshattered former self and compensate for what he or she has suffered. Many look to knowledge of the trauma and its effects on their parent in order to interpret the meaning of their parent's current emotional states and behaviors.

When there is little communication about the parent's trauma, children split off what they do know along with the fantasies they have generated to fill in gaps into a dissociated part of themselves. Later events in their own life can break open what's split off and throw them into bewildering and upsetting feelings and images that flood their bodies and minds.

For psychoanalysts, these later events importantly include the events that transpire in psychoanalysis with patients. What is unnamed or unresolved in patients "goes in search of an echo, in this improbable other [the analyst], of what official history has marginalized or trivialized, evoking in the analyst details and anecdotes that have been unclaimed, even in his or her own analysis" (Davoine & Gaudilliére, 2004, p. 11). A remnant of something that I hadn't fully claimed was stirred in the consultation group. It took full form in and after my day in the courtroom.

* * *

My father was diagnosed with Alzheimer's disease in 1992 at the age of 71. He died 13 years later. It was a slow, insidious decline he suffered. Ironically, and thankfully, he discovered an inner peace that we had never known him to have. As he mellowed more and more and his memory increasingly failed him, he sometimes talked about things in ways he would not have before he got sick. One day in the middle period of his Alzheimer's, he talked to me a little about his father's murder.

He said, "Dr. Gruness [the psychiatrist my father saw] wondered if I felt guilty, but I don't really think so. My father knew what he was getting into, and he knew what was going to happen. I don't know why he didn't just give the business up. It just wasn't that important. He should have said the hell with it and kissed it goodbye and given it to those guys. That's what I would have done. But that wasn't the way he was structured. He was too proud to do that. And so they killed him. My brother James was in the business with him, but I don't know how much of a help he was. And my father's plan was that I'd go into the business, too, which I wasn't really very enthused about. So ...."

"I've wondered not about your feeling guilty but your feeling angry and helpless," I said.

"Yeah, and after he was shot that wasn't the end of it. He was in the hospital for another 3 months, and it was a big hassle. It fell to me to take care of things. I was the one who was there the most, and they had a policeman at one end of the hall and one at the other, but that didn't stop them, so ... well, I don't mean to burden you."

2 September 11, 2001*

September 12

I waited through the night along with 12 other psychologists at Seward Park High School in Chinatown, just blocks from what is now being called Ground Zero. The Red Cross was expecting upwards of a thousand survivors of the attack on the World Trade Center to be pulled out of the rubble and brought there for triage. Hundreds of cots had been set up in the school gymnasium, but only two people came for shelter all night: a homeless man, and a man whose girlfriend had thrown him out of their apartment after an argument.

September 13

There was a posting today on the listserv of the candidates, graduates, and faculty of the NYU Postdoctoral Program in Psychotherapy and Psychoanalysis. Psychologists are urgently needed to do employee assistance work with businesses that had offices in or near the World Trade Center. I called, and on Monday morning I am to go to the temporary headquarters of the Manhattan Investment Corporation at 44th Street and Avenue of the Americas.

---

*An earlier version of this chapter appeared in the *Northwest Review*, 41(1), 2003.

September 17

Met with a group of 30 Manhattan Investment Corporation employees. I said to them, "Everyone is asking how they can help, and there is so little we can do. But one thing we can do, and that we shouldn't underestimate the power of, is to listen to each other, to listen to what happened to each other on September 11. And one way to help ourselves is to tell the story of what has happened to us." One by one, these 30 people told the story of what had happened to them.

Many thought it was an earthquake when the first plane struck; one woman saw a fallen woman being trampled on; another said that she froze at her desk and had to be pulled out of her chair by coworkers; a man who'd moved from Missouri just the week before said he roamed the streets lost after getting separated from his friend when the dust ball hit; two buddies made their way to Washington Square Park, bought a six-pack, shared it on a bench in the park, and watched the two towers fall; an intern ran past a burning airplane seat cushion, a chef's hat, and a Louis Vuitton purse lying on the sidewalk; a woman told of people yelling for the Staten Island ferry to leave behind others who were running toward it when the dust ball hit; many wore orange life vests on boat trips home from work that day; one man witnessed a passenger jump off a ferry in the middle of New York Harbor with people screaming for the captain to go back and get him while others panicked, sure he'd left an explosive behind on the ferry; another tried to no avail to stop a pregnant woman from going back into the World Trade Center to get her purse; many were covered with ash and soot; one woman started to scream at her husband to stop laughing only to realize his body was shuddering in sobs; a woman from human resources yelled, "I'm so mad all this is happening and those fuckers, they're living right in the middle of us. Those fuckers live in my neighborhood in New Jersey"; a vice president opened a bottle of Jack Daniels and drank until he passed out; a middle-aged man filled grocery carts with food and milk and water and cooked soul food for days for his family and neighbors; a secretary said what did it matter anymore if a file was color-coded red or green or blue or yellow; one man said he now runs out of his house to search the sky to see if he is safe every time a plane goes by; others said they don't think they will ever get the sound of the explosion out of their heads; many saw men and women who had jumped flying past the floor-to-ceiling windows of their offices. Eyes reddened and jaws clenched;

men and women wept openly; people listened quietly, almost reverently. We listened for 2 hours.

* * *

I picked up a hot pretzel and Diet Coke at a street vendor on the way to the Village. I had six patients to see in my office, and didn't know how I'd do it. I was exhausted. As I walked toward the subway I felt dizzy, like the ground might come out from under me. The top of my head was numb.

* * *

Roger. He looked angry when he walked in. As he was lying down on the couch, he began, "I know I'm in the minority and it isn't a popular opinion to hold, but who do we think we are? Why do we think this happened to us? We act as if we're blameless. We ought to be asking why, really asking, why these people attacked us."

He went on in anger about people hanging pictures of missing loved ones on the walls of the subway stations. "Why are they doing that?" he asked. "Do they really think anyone is still alive? It's absurd. No one survived. It's ridiculous that people are putting those pictures up." I didn't understand. This was so unlike him. As he ranted on about the pictures, a mild outrage rose in me.

And then he said he didn't know why he was so mad about it, and I asked, "Why do you think you are?"

He paused, then said, "Because I don't know if anyone cares enough about me that they'd do that for me if I were missing."

I involuntarily glanced at his right leg. It was in a metal brace. It had been since he was a little boy and contracted polio. His walk is labored and tortured looking. Growing up, the neighborhood kids shunned and teased him, and he had no friends at school. We were both silent for a time, and then his chest started heaving in a kind of silent sobbing.

* * *

Helen. She told me about talking to her mother on the phone that morning before heading to her office. She said, "I didn't know what I needed. I just knew I felt agitated. And then my mother said, 'Oh, honey, I'm so sorry you have to go through this,' and I knew I needed comfort."

How amazing, I thought, that Helen can find comfort from her mother. It wouldn't have been possible a year ago. And I thought of my own mother, feeling the comfort along with Helen, and the wish to talk to my own mother, the comfort of that.

* * *

Lucinda. She feels so victimized by others, and today she cried like a child, asking, "Why do they hate us? Why do people hate us?" She talked of her fear for her life, that the attacks would mushroom and we would all be killed. She didn't understand why other people hate us. I felt overwhelmed and mostly listened. The more she talked, the calmer she got, and then she said, "I always feel so unwanted. It's like I don't know how else to feel. I have an image of a woman, bent and doubled over, hugging herself. How did that little girl I was grow up into such a frightened woman? I think, but in the doubling over it's like the girl is in the woman."

"A chance for rebirth," I said.

* * *

Lisa. She looked as cool and imperturbable as usual and didn't mention anything about the World Trade Center until halfway through the session. Then, in the middle of a story about herself and her boyfriend walking down the street, she said, "I'm so afraid of car bombs now. We were walking down University Place, and a car alarm went off. I jumped. I thought it was a car bomb. I never thought of not living in New York," she said. "But these days I think about it. I don't take the subway anymore. I take cabs or walk, but I can't stop thinking of car bombs when I'm walking down the street."

* * *

Both Zena and Fiona spoke of feeling a "desperate need" today; that was the phrase they both used.

* * *

Zena. She swears she will never get involved in another relationship again, but said she has been feeling "a desperate need" and started having sexual fantasies this week for the first time since her last breakup. They are of me and a former lover of hers. Her voice was filled with anxiety, and she said, "Tell me it's okay. I need you to tell me it's okay."

"I think it's your feeling of desperate need you're worried about being okay," I said.

* * *

Fiona. She doesn't wear clothes as much as costumes. Today she was dressed in a black skirt and blouse, black tights and shoes, and a black broad-brimmed hat with a red rose pinned to the brim. She said she feels like she's living on another planet from her friends. They're not as sad or frightened, or as grief-stricken, about the attack on New York, her home. She said, "It's like a death. You want to be with the people you love, and you want to feel secure in those relationships. I just want someone to put their arms around me and tell me everything's going to be all right, but it's frightening to want because when I want I really, really want. It's what I have to have. I feel a desperate need."

Neither was conscious of any connection between this feeling of desperate need and the world situation, the fear and sadness and destruction we are living amidst. It seemed so clear to me, and when I made the connection they both had an awareness of it close at hand.

When Fiona left I became aware of how much my back and the backs of my legs ached, and all I wanted to do was go home, but I needed a few minutes for reflection. The isolation, the fear, the terror, the need of another, the need to feel safe in the closeness and comfort of another, and the healing power of kindness and love are at the center of our psyches now. So much foundational has come undone. Now there is the possibility to bind it, to weave it together differently this time. The primitive terrors each of us faced early on in life are thrust upon us, and the fundamental sense of safety in the world we attained is ruptured. We reach in need for love to heal and grow anew—a second chance.

September 21

Before getting on the subway, I stopped at Union Square. People milled around the Square. Most had a dazed look in their eyes. Others looked desperate or sad. There was a man, with a beer belly that protruded out over his belt, dressed in jeans and a short-sleeve, red plaid shirt. His blonde hair was thinning and receding. He'd set up a microphone and had taken over the corner above the subway entrance at 14th Street and Union Square West. He said he was a minister from New Jersey and he and his staff had come into the city to be with the people of New York, to show their solidarity with us, to share Jesus with us.

Off to his side stood a card table stacked high with paperback copies of the Bible. A sign said they were free for anyone to take.

I joined the milling crowd, passing silently by one picture after another posted up on lampposts or taped down to the sidewalk. Vigil lights and bouquets of flowers from the green grocer, some with their plastic wrap left on, were placed in rings around the pictures of the missing on the sidewalk. They were so young. Most had birth dates in the late 1960s or the 1970s. "Missing," the signs said, Xeroxed photos of smiling young adults with fresh, well-fed faces.

At the bottom of the stairs to the park on 14th Street, there were three people beating drums. One was a woman with her head shaved, dressed in the flowing crimson robe of a Buddhist nun; one, a heavy-set woman in a floppy straw hat sitting on a wooden stool; and the third, an American Indian with a long ponytail dressed in blue jeans and a navy blue T-shirt. He and the Buddhist nun sat with their legs tucked underneath them on the sidewalk. Each held a round, delicate-looking drum attached to a long handle. They beat their drums in unison with a thin stick—one long beat, three short beats, over and over again. I stood watching them, mesmerized by the sound of the drumbeat, the sight of their still presences. They kept their eyes cast either down to the ground or up to the sky, absorbed in the beat they drummed.

I wanted to know where I could get a drum and join them. The relentless, wordless beating of life was insistent. It was all that there really was. It was all that we could say or know. It seemed more real, more true, more powerful than anything else I could think to do in the face of September 11. If I had followed my instincts, I would have asked to join with them, and I would spend these days on Union Square, sitting on the ground, beating on a drum—one long beat, three short ones, over and over again.

September 26

Matt was the first person I saw today. He hadn't shaved in several days, and he wore the same brown corduroy pants and navy blue T-shirt he'd been wearing all week. His hair was dry and laid flat on his head instead of gelled and styled back like it usually was. He jumped every time a subway went by, its rumble rising through the sidewalk grates up through my office window. The sound is so faint I've never noticed it before, but Matt jumped and said it sounds like the roar of a train racing right toward him now.

Each day this week, he'd talked a little more about moments of September 11. He was in the lobby of the World Trade Center, registering for a conference in the hotel, when the first plane struck; dodged falling glass; threw himself to the ground underneath a registration table; and waited to leave in the lobby along with everyone else. A woman outside had been sliced in half by a broken window flying through the air—that was the rumor, anyhow, that spread through the pandemonium of the crowd inside. They were safer inside than out, they were told. And then the second plane hit and "all hell broke loose," Matt said. "People charged the doors and ran for their lives. I ran a ways, then thought, 'Go back. You have to go back.' I thought there had to be lots of people who were going to need help and I was all right and I could help, so I turned and started running back against the crowd and that's when I saw the people flying through the air—these men and women wildly swinging their arms hurtling towards the ground." Matt's face contorted, and he held his breath to keep from crying but then exhaled a huge breath and started sobbing. Through his sobs he said, "And do you know what, Dr. Ragen? People don't splatter when they hit the ground. They crack. They crack apart at the limbs," he said and sunk his head to his chest, his chest and back shuddering with sobs.

Tears trickled down my cheeks, and I felt nauseous and I wanted to reach out and hold Matt. I thought of his mother and how she was dead and that Matt didn't have a mother to hold him and how he'd often said that I reminded him of his mother—that she was strong, smart, and athletic. And then I saw an image of Matt at his mother's funeral singing the "Ave Maria" and thought of how when we first met he proudly told me, "There wasn't a dry eye in the house when I finished—except for mine." Matt had never once cried the whole time his mother was sick and dying of cancer. He'd even thought no one at school knew his mother was dying, even though a few months before she died she came to watch him in a play, and she was wearing a wig and walking with a cane and had wasted away into a thin woman with dark circles under her eyes.

September 27, 4 a.m.

A lot of people are awake. Many apartments along 90th Street have lights on or the hazy, bluish glare of television sets in dark rooms. I think we are behind the rest of the country in thinking of the future, and I am glad. We're still absorbing the shock and trauma with only glimmers of thoughts about the future. It feels overwhelming to think of the future, yet oddly comforting to stay in the present trauma.

I wonder sometimes if my work simply provides an illusion that I am doing something in the face of the powerlessness that is so much of the reality of the situation. Sometimes I wonder that, but most of the time I see the power of listening, really listening to others—like with Matt today. I hate the waves of feeling passing through me these days—fear, despair, sadness, terror, shock, isolation—but when I disconnect from my feelings I feel like a zombie, and that feels much worse than feeling. When I wake up is when I sometimes feel real despair and fear for the future. Most often, though, I wake up in terror. It's there before I even remember or have any conscious thought of what is happening these days. I wake up into it, like it's been there all along. I'm tired at night but don't want to go to bed. I'm vaguely restless and want to stay up until I've read or done something gratifying and satisfying, but nothing is. I fall asleep but more often than not wake up a few hours later—like now—toss and turn, then finally get up and read. I try the *New Yorker*, *Tennis Magazine*, catalogues. I can't concentrate on anything. Nothing holds my attention. I look at that day's *New York Times* sitting on the top of the pile of newspapers in the corner of the living room, but won't let myself pick it up. It would only keep me up longer to start reading about September 11. I want to talk to people and do. It is comforting on one level and helps me feel secure, but more and more I feel alienation underneath when I'm talking with others. It's like I can't express in social conversation the core of what I'm experiencing. There is a raw core I long to speak from, to speak into a quiet, open space where it is simply received and absorbed and someone sits with me and just takes it in and holds it. I feel like we all need to be quiet. I keep thinking, "There are too many words," and recall a line about words from T. S. Eliot's poem "Ash Wednesday" (1930/1963): "These wings are no longer wings to fly, but merely vans to beat the air" (p. 84).

September 31

On the way to the bank today, I walked past an old couple on University Avenue. The woman had a handkerchief over her mouth, and the man held his hand over his. At first I thought it was because of the air. People are still walking the streets downtown with scarves or handkerchiefs over their mouths to filter out the pollution and stench that hangs in the air, a stench like burning rubber that some speculate is the odor of burning flesh. But as they got closer I saw that they were both sobbing, holding each other up, walking arm in arm down the street. Someone must have died, I thought, and an awful pain went through me. A block away I walked past a group of workmen speaking something that sounded like Czechoslovakian around their van. An attractive young woman in a tight skirt walked by. The men ogled her. One who had a lewd look on his face said something to the others, and they all laughed. Then he let out a catcall at the woman. It was like someone lit a gas-soaked rag inside of me, as a rage flashed through me and I found myself walking straight toward the man who'd made the joke, staring right at his crotch. He didn't see me coming at first, but when he did his lewd look turned to surprise. "We don't do that in America!" I yelled at him and walked away fast and into the Chase Bank on the corner. By the time I used the ATM and walked out the men were gone and I had kind of caught up with myself, thrown by what I'd done, and asked myself, "What was that? What happened to you that you did that?" And immediately I saw the grieving old couple in my mind.

October 5

It's Saturday, and I woke to terror and got up and began to read the paper, the "Books" section of the *Times*, but started to cry and could not stop, and thought I needed to get away, to rest, to be quiet, away from anything having to do with the attack on the World Trade Center, to go somewhere that is healing. And I went to the phone and called Charlotte at the O'Brien Mercy Center, one of the Sisters of Mercy at their conference and retreat center in Rhode Island. I got a recorded message telling me to call back Monday through Friday between 9:00 a.m. and 5:00 p.m. There was an emergency number, but I didn't think I was an emergency.

October 7

I felt like a robot when I walked out of the South American division of the Manhattan Investment Corporation today. They'd asked me to be available to meet with any of the 12 employees from that division who wanted to talk. Beforehand I met with Dominic, the head of the division. As we sat there talking I wondered how it was that he was head of this division, and was struck by how I thought he could be handsome but wasn't. He is tall, has thick salt-and-pepper hair and a nicely shaped face and eyes, but he seems to have no vigor or vitality. "Kind of mousy" ran through my head. We set up a process for employees to be able to come and talk with me if they wanted to, then Dominic left. It was already 2:30 in the afternoon. Four or five people came to see me. The last one's name was Abel. His blue shirt was wet with perspiration under his arms. His face seemed like a mask at first, but then softened and became more animated as we talked. Abel was wound so tight that I was concerned about him. He was very worried because he wasn't concentrating well, couldn't remember things, and was terrified he'd make a mistake on one of his accounts and be fired. He had a lot of medical bills for the therapy his son needed because of his speech disability, and they weren't covered by insurance; in addition, almost all his savings had been in stocks, so he'd lost a lot of money in the market since the attack. I told him no one was concentrating or remembering things well right now; that was one impact of the trauma. He said I didn't understand. He'd only started this job a year ago, and he'd been having some trouble. He wasn't picking things up as fast as he should be. He got up every morning at 5:00, went and worked out, and was at his desk by 7:00. Most nights he got home by 10:00, so he could see his son before he went to bed.

Dominic came in to see me after Abel left. He asked how it had gone. I said it went well. Several people had come in to see me. "I hope they used the time well," he said.

"People are still very upset and needing to talk about what's happened to them," I said.

"We're going to have to let Abel go," Dominic said. I let out a sigh and shifted in my seat, putting my head in my hand, but said nothing. "It's unfortunate," he went on. "No one works harder than he does, but he just isn't performing."

I asked if the department had tried to help him. He said they had. "He just can't connect the dots," Dominic said.

"What a shame—someone so bright but who lacks what's needed for this job," I said, knowing from Abel he had gotten an MBA from Harvard.

"I'm not sure how bright he is," Dominic said and shrugged. "HR has asked us to wait a few months before we fire him. He'll never find a job, not in the state things will be in now."

Dominic went on to tell me he was worried his people would not be "psychologically strong enough after the trauma of the attack on the World Trade Center to do their jobs." He thought they'd need a different kind of person in the bureau now. "We need sharks," he said. "The South American economy is going to be devastated now."

Dominic explained that what his firm did was go into South America, buy companies, improve them, and then sell them at a profit for the bank. "I could make the wealth of a lifetime in the next 12 to 24 months. We have a low base salary and make most of our money from getting a percentage of each deal we make. The money each of us makes is pooled, and as a group each of us gets a percentage of that. Now I've got one guy saying he's never going to fly again. I had one of my best employees closing a deal in Colombia this week. I told her I wanted her to get the company there to make two more concessions. She said she wouldn't do it. She said it wasn't fair and she wasn't going to put her credibility and reputation on the line, and if I wanted those concessions I'd have to send someone else to close the deal. So I sent someone else and he got the concessions I wanted, which showed it was an achievable goal. You know," he said, "I'm from Italy. We're used to terrorism over there. People here just aren't used to it."

October 8

I woke up with that robotic-like feeling again, that hollowed-out, metallic-like feeling, like the tin man who lost his heart. I thought, "That's it," and got out of bed and called Charlotte at the Sisters of Mercy Retreat Center. I got right through to her. She thought I was calling about a workshop we were going to give together at the center and started to apologize for not having called me sooner, and I told her that was all right, that's not why I was calling. I needed to get away for a few days, I said, and asked if I could come to the center for a long weekend and if I could talk to her. "My gosh," she said. "You're in New York. I was so focused on the workshop I didn't even think to ask how you are in the midst of all that's happening there."

"It's okay," I said, and Charlotte told me of course, to come, and she would see me.

The Sisters of Mercy have been a source of strength to me for a long time. Taught by them in high school, I saw what a difference they could make in people's lives. When I asked myself at the end of college what I wanted to do with my life, I thought I'd like to be a Sister of Mercy. I entered the community, and although I left 7 years later, it was with an enduring gratitude to and respect for them.

October 11

When Marshall saw me standing at the Metro North information booth, he said, "Glory be to God," then made the sign of the cross. He was a short, stooped man in his late 70s or so. He wore a grimy brown and white striped polo shirt. He was a good foot shorter than I but insisted on carrying my bags to the cab. I was an hour late. When I'd called to make arrangements for a cab, I'd looked down at the schedule and told the woman at the cab company I'd be there at 11:21 a.m. instead of 12:21 p.m. I'd been thinking of taking the train that got in at 11:21 but decided to sleep in and go a little later.

Somehow I'd gotten confused.

Earlier in the week I'd gotten on the subway in Chinatown. It was a 15-minute ride to my office. Several minutes into the ride, I found myself up in the air looking out over water and thinking, "It's like being on the el in Chicago." Only I wasn't in Chicago. I was in New York City and on my way to Brooklyn. I'd taken the 6 train going south instead of north. Forty-five minutes later I arrived in my office, 15 minutes late for my first appointment.

The taxi stunk. I opened both back windows. We were on I-95 headed south from Providence, Rhode Island. A cold breeze came in and I could hear the rumbling sound of the cab's muffler going, but it beat the smell. Marshall turned and said, "Whoa," and then asked if I could smell the paint. "I sure can," I said, relieved though somewhat suspicious about it being paint. He said he'd just gotten the dashboard of his taxi painted.

Marshall was a demolitions expert in World War II. His job was to go ahead of the Allied troops and blow up tall buildings that snipers could perch on top of when the Allies marched into their towns. He said he knew exactly how to take care of Osama bin Laden. He'd tie him up in explosives and let them rip, he said. "His people will get him," Marshall said. "They'll turn on him—just like they did on Mussolini. You know how Mussolini died, don't you?"

"No. How did he die?" I asked as Marshall swerved back onto the highway from an exit ramp he had mistakenly headed onto. I noticed the lenses of Marshall's glasses from the back seat. They were thick lenses set in heavy brown frames, and the lenses were all smudged. I leaned over to try to look through them at the road. They were so smudged I didn't know how Marshall could see out of them. Marshall told me that Mussolini fled to the mountains, but his people followed him and found him there and stoned him to death.

"They'll turn on him. There's a price on his head, a big price. Forty-five million I heard. Whoa! But he's not in Afghanistan anymore. No sirree!" Marshall said.

"Where do you think he is?" I asked.

"He's in Iran by now. I'd bet my life on it. But they'll get him. Forty-five million is a lot of money."

We turned off I-95 to Old Highway 1, and as we got close to the retreat center Marshall told me he was born and raised Catholic. He was close to Jesus, he said, but not a very good Catholic. He was from a devout Italian family. Every Sunday he'd go off with the other guys his age, pretending they were going to Mass.

"There was one Sunday a year I went, though," Marshall said.

I figured it must have been Christmas or Easter.

"That was Palm Sunday. I'd go and get a palm so I could bring one home with me!" Marshall chuckled, and then said, "Ah, that wasn't nice of me. That wasn't nice at all, but I was just a kid, not doing anything I was supposed to do. My mother used to hit me on the side of the head with the palm of her hand. She'd say, 'Marshall, you think you're something else,' then hit me and say, 'See! You're not such a big shot.'"

As we pulled around the circle drive to the front door of the retreat center, Marshall said, "This place is beautiful."

"Isn't it?" I said.

Marshall was quiet a moment, then said, "The hand of God has touched this place."

I said, "Yeah, that's what it's like when you're here."

Marshall got out to get my bags from the trunk and said, "I know. I can feel it."

* * *

The woman who met me at the door introduced herself as Sister Suzanne. She was a short, strong-looking woman in her late 50s. She offered to take one of my bags and led me to a room that looked out on Rhode Island Sound. It was a cold, gray day. She said, "It's supposed to be a nice day tomorrow. You probably need to sleep today anyhow." She left, and I unpacked my bags and thought about when I'd go to the chapel or out for a walk. The backs of my legs ached and I felt exhausted, but I didn't want to waste the little time I had there sleeping. Then I thought of her saying, "You probably need to sleep today," and I let myself lie down. Two hours later, I woke refreshed.

October 12

Marshall came back today. I saw the yellow cab sitting at the front door to the center as I rode up the long driveway on the 15-speed Raleigh I'd rented in town for the weekend. The driver's door opened, and there was Marshall dropping off a woman. Just as he finished handing her her bags from the trunk, I pulled up. Marshall's face lit up. "I was hoping I'd see you," he said.

It had been kind of a hard day for me. I had angry dreams, and I woke up feeling angry. Then I became aware of a feeling of sadness in my heart. This morning I sat out on the bench on the knoll overlooking the beach, my feet dangling over the split-rail fence, wishing I'd brought my sunglasses because the reflection of the sun off the Sound was so glaring, wearing the hood of my jacket pulled up against the October breeze.

"God is the only reality in which all other reality takes place." These words from Thomas Merton (1962, p. 226) stuck with me from what I'd just read. "God is the only reality in which all other reality takes place." I moved into those words. They took me down, deep into the center where there is peace and silence and tranquility—the place in which all other reality can take place. I felt my self taking place, my thoughts and feelings taking place in God—in this peace. The anger came back, but the peace was encapsulated. Angry thoughts, nagging annoying thoughts, skittered through my head. They were there, but didn't touch the peace and silence, the presence below, the core. The angry thoughts felt burdensome, but separate—a separate, more superficial reality that stood outside the silence within.

Later in the morning, I'd gone for a bike ride to try to shake off some of the anger and was feeling pretty good again by the time I saw Marshall.

"You can really feel the road under you on a bike, can't you?" Marshall said.

"Yeah."

"So, how's it going, your retreat and all?" he asked.

"Pretty well," I said, and asked if he'd like to see the grounds. He pulled over his cab to the side of the circle drive, and we walked toward the beach.

"Beautiful, just beautiful," Marshall kept saying.

When we started to pass the statue of Joseph and Jesus, Marshall said, "Hold on," and walked over, blessed himself, and knelt with his head bowed for a minute or two. Even though it was a cold October day, Marshall was still wearing the soiled, striped, short-sleeved polo shirt he picked me up in at the train station. As he knelt he pulled his brown tweed Ivy League cap off his head. When he got up he said, "You remember I told you I never was a very good Catholic but I was always close to Jesus? I always felt him right here with me," Marshall said, pounding his fist on his heart. "There were many times I know he saved me when we were over in Germany. One night in particular I remember. We were coming up on the town hall of this small town. There was no one around. It was the middle of the night. We had no reason to think there were any German soldiers within a hundred miles of the place, so I guess we were a little too sure of ourselves. We walked right down the middle of the main street toward the town hall to set up the demolition. The next thing I know a bullet whizzes past my ear, this far away." Marshall showed me, with his fingers only a couple of inches from his head. "The bullet was only this far away. That was Jesus. I know it was. There's no reason that bullet should have missed me. I was an easy target. I owe my life to Jesus. I really do."

We rounded the corner around the front of the house where the beach was. The sun was just starting to set. The trees had lost most of their leaves, and up against the background of the crimson sky the pattern of branches and limbs was an intricate weave. Marshall took off his glasses.

"Huh!" he said. "That's beautiful, but all I have to do to make it more beautiful is take my glasses off. It's like one of those impressionistic paintings," he said.

It was getting close to dinnertime. I told Marshall I was sorry I didn't have more time to walk the grounds with him, but dinner was at 6:30.

He was quick to say, "No. No. That's fine. I didn't want to bother you."

"You're not bothering me, Marshall. It was good to see you."

"Yeah, well, like I said I was hoping I would run into you."

As Marshall got into his cab, I said, "Thanks, Marshall. Really, thanks."

"I'll be here at 9 o'clock sharp for you on Tuesday," Marshall said and drove away.

October 13, Afternoon

Charlotte is the embodiment of what my image of a New England woman is. She is tall and lean and to the point, and she has a warmth that does not gush but brews just beneath the surface. When I arrived at her office, she was at her computer, her desk filled with papers she was working on and a worn New Jerusalem Bible.

As she turned to greet me, I saw the look of concern on her face. "You look tired," she said.

"I am," I said and began to cry before I'd even sat down. "I need someone to listen," I said.

"Go ahead," she said and nodded.

"I keep thinking I'm going to turn the corner, that any day I'm going to start feeling like myself again, but it isn't happening. I guess that's the worst part—not feeling like myself. I can take feeling the waves of anger, sadness, fear, terror, the nausea and dizziness that come, but it's this awful feeling underneath that seems to be getting stronger—this feeling of alienation inside of me, between me and me, between me and others, that's really getting to me. It feels so not me. At its worst I have this robotic-like feeling, at best it's this undercurrent of feeling alienated—kind of like I'm actually living beside myself. That's the worst part," I said.

I went on to tell Charlotte about how I woke to terror, couldn't stop crying when I got up in the mornings, was restless and agitated at night, and woke up in the middle of the night unable to go back to sleep. I went on to tell her about the bank, about the grieving old couple on University Place and how I lost it with the workman, about the night in the high school gymnasium when no one came, about how hard it is to listen hour after hour to patients, but how hard it is to talk about anything else, how meaningless it seems, how scared I am, how scared we all are we'll be attacked again. I cried and couldn't stop crying, and near the end I stopped and said, "What's wrong with me?"

"What's wrong with you?" Charlotte said.

I waited for her answer.

"You're terrified," she said. "You're terrified and you feel powerless. The terror you know you feel. But the one feeling I didn't hear you mention at all as you talked about these past weeks was feeling powerless. I think you're fighting the realization of how powerless you feel, and it's making things worse. I think that's what's making you feel estranged."

October 13, Evening

Tonight I sat in chapel, two pillows under me and two up against the wall to support my back. There was a tan glen plaid cashmere throw on the bench next to me. I tossed it over my shoulders and closed my eyes and sat with the feeling of powerlessness, sinking down into it, and letting myself fill with it—a raw, pure feeling of powerlessness. There was a hush in the chapel, and the October wind whistled through the trees outside. The anger was gone. The fear was gone. Sitting on the floor in the chapel, I felt only the feeling of powerlessness. It felt good. It felt comforting in some strange way. Everything was still inside me except for the feeling of powerlessness. It felt oddly liberating.

October 14, Morning

I've come to hate the banner that hangs from ceiling to floor behind the altar. It's a painting of a huge white rose emerging out of a dissonant, dark background of streaks of black and gray and purple. When I was here this summer, I liked it. I liked the sense of the paradox of death and resurrection it evoked, the new life that can come out of darkness, but now it is too much. I know the darkness and devastation all too well, too daily, and I don't want to see any more of it. I wish they would take the banner down.

October 14, Afternoon

The leadership team of the Sisters of Mercy has issued a statement about September 11. There's a stack of them printed up on a table at the entrance to the chapel. It says, in part,

> While we join our voice in the national mourning, we cannot join the cacophony of voices demanding retaliation and revenge.... It is our deepest prayer that we, who have so recently experienced the destructive power of hatred, will not now emulate it. We join our voices with those who are calling for a reexamination of the roots of the anger which has erupted against us—poverty, injustice, and hopelessness—and our complicity in these root circumstances; for deep and careful self-reflection as a nation; for messages to the President of the United States and members of Congress expressing a desire for a response which will incite peace rather than war.

I sit with these words. It is good to be here.

October 14, on the Beach

I lie in the crevice between two granite rocks at the end of the beach. The voices of young boys and the thud of a soccer ball waft over the dune grass from the field next door. Waves ripple over rocks on the shore.

Black birds perch in the maple tree. A statue of Mary, arms spread open, stands over the garden by the labyrinth. An airplane passes overhead, and for a moment the protrusions from the front of the wings of the plane look like guns to me, but, then I realize they are propellers. All the same, the dark rain shower against the hazy orange sky off on the western shore makes me wonder if the twin towers are still smoldering. I hear the rumble of a plane I cannot see and wonder if it is an F-15. The waves lap against the shore. Black crows squawk at each other in the fir tree. "We haven't lost because we've kept trying," Eliot says in *Dry Salvages* (1944, p. 45). A desolate thought. It's more than that. The dust of the devastation leads us to the divine in the innermost reaches of our heart.

October 15, Dawn

I woke up in the middle of the night and realized I felt safe. An active, palpable, almost tangible feeling of safety filled me. I lay in bed trying to stay awake as long as I could, to feel safe as long as possible. This morning I woke to "I can't go back. Not yet. It's too soon," urgent words in my head. Everything in me wants to stay here, just for another day—maybe 2. I actually thought for a minute about whether there was any way I could do that, whether I could really justifiably do that—reschedule my patients to later in the week—and then I remembered I had an appointment with a patient who has moved out of the country. She is in town for 10 days, and today is our last appointment before she leaves.

October 15, Morning

I am outside waiting on the bench on the circle drive and hear the rumble of Marshall's muffler coming down the road.

3 Longing*

There is a small book with a rust-colored cover in my bookcase. It is titled *The Story of a Soul*. Inside the cover, in strong, bold handwriting in the thick ink of a fountain pen, is written "To Therese Ragen" and below that, underlined, "June 1, 1956." It is my father's handwriting. I was 6 years old, and I have responded to him with two scrawls of lime green crayon on the inside of the cover, each a free-flowing green line extending out, then back on itself, then out again.

When I was born, the Rh factor had only recently been discovered. My mother was Rh-negative, and had I been born Rh-positive there might have been complications in the delivery. During my mother's pregnancy my parents prayed to St. Therese that the delivery would go well. I was born Rh-negative, and my father, who my mother said had a strong devotion to St. Therese of Lisieux, suggested they name me after her.

St. Therese herself was named after St. Teresa of Avila, one of the great mystics of the Catholic Church. Both were Carmelite nuns, a cloistered, contemplative order—Teresa of Avila in the 1500s and Therese of Lisieux in the 1800s. And both were instructed by their spiritual directors to write the stories of their spiritual lives. Therese of Lisieux's

*This chapter originally appeared in *Contemporary Psychoanalysis*, 43(4), 2007. Reprinted with permission.

(1899/1995) is *The Story of a Soul.* Teresa of Avila's (1577/1961) is *The Interior Castle*, the castle her metaphor for the soul. She wrote,

> I began to think of the soul as if it were a castle made of a single diamond or of very clear crystal ... which contains numerous mansions, some above, others below, others at each side; and in the centre and midst of them all is the chiefest mansion where the most secret things pass between God and the soul. (pp. 28–29)

As she passes through each level, Teresa's understandings of self and of God simultaneously deepen. For Teresa, God lives within. She points to the idea that God lives within halfway through her autobiography: "Before, I was writing about my life, but now I have been writing about the life God has been living in me." (Teresa of Avila, 1960, p. 220)

Therese of Lisieux (1899/1995) had a longing about her vocation, a sense of wanting more. She said, "I feel the call of more vocations still: I want to be a warrior, a priest, an apostle, a doctor of the church, a martyr" (p.187). Simply, she wrote, "I long to bring light to souls" (p. 188). And then, again, "I have found my vocation at last. It is love.... I will be love" (p. 190).

She had a vision of the Church:

> I saw that the Church must have a *heart,* that this heart must be on fire with love. I saw that it was love alone which moved her members, and that were this love to fail, apostles would no longer spread the Gospel, and martyrs would refuse to shed their blood. I saw that all vocations are summed up in love, and that love is all in all, embracing every time and place because it is eternal. (p. 190)

Love ... souls ... these are not words in my psychoanalytic vocabulary. These are not realities through which we work and speak and have our psychoanalytic being—not often, anyhow. I miss these words, these realities. I miss them in and with my patients, in my colleagues and myself. Rank talked about love. Freud talked about the soul. How and when did we lose these parts of ourselves?

Freud used the term *seelig* in his work. Bruno Bettelheim (1983) claimed that the correct translation of *seelig* is "structure of the soul" and points out that Freud referred to himself as a "midwife of the soul." Unfortunately, in the English translation of Freud's work, *seelig* was translated as "Metal apparatus" or "Mental organization" (p. 71). And Otto Rank (1968), whose voice is barely a whisper now, saw psychoanalysis as a science of relation. (How like Therese of Lisieux, who reported that at the end of one particularly dry meditation the words that came into her mind were "Here is the master I give you to teach you all you have to do. I want you to study the Book of Life, which contains 'the' *Science of Love*" [p. 183].) Rank believed that the power of the creative will was "equal to the influences of the outer environment and the inner instinctual life" (Menaker, 1982, p. 50). Whereas Freud offered a historical-causal interpretation of life, Rank emphasized a genetic-constructive interpretation in which the active inherent forces of an individual's creative will, strivings for growth, and hidden potentials play a major role. Psychoanalysis helps patients find "the divine spark" within, according to Rank.

Carl Jung's (Ulanov, 1996) work focused on the Self, which he saw as the center of the psyche, transcending and including both the conscious and the unconscious. The Self is that in us that knows about the Transcendent, that in us that knows about God or whatever we experience as ultimate reality. Jung and Rank were both members of Freud's inner circle whose thinking gradually grew away from Freud's. Their differences with Freud culminated painfully in their being ostracized by Freud and the psychoanalytic establishment. Both Jung and Rank concerned themselves much more with spirit and soul than Freud did. Freudians and those of us from psychoanalytic groups that later split off from classical Freudian psychoanalysis—object relations theorists, Kleinians, interpersonalists, and relational thinkers—all suffer the loss of these now dissociated voices, parts of our own spirits and souls exiled with them.

* * *

It has been almost a day since the Triborough Bridge disappeared from view. It had just gotten dark when the snow began. It came down lightly at first, but within the hour the lights of the bridge were gone and all you could see was the dark night, snow blowing across it. This morning when I awoke, I could make out a faint outline of the road across the water but nothing else. But now even that is gone again.

The East River is choppy, a dark, dull gray today. A lone bird flies by. The tiny island just offshore grows less and less visible. A foghorn blows as a boat emerges out of the mist. A man in a red jacket and blue jeans is on the East River promenade on cross-country skis. His movements are labored and jagged. He doesn't seem to know how to glide. He lifts his feet, trying to walk along in his skis.

As I sit, mulling over Jung's, Freud's, and Rank's ideas and watching the snow fall, my mind drifts to Ben. When he first came to treatment 2 years ago, Ben recalled spending a year in India after graduation from college. "I was trying to find myself," he said. "But, actually, I didn't look too hard."

Fifteen years have passed. Ben is still trying to find himself, and I think he is on the verge of beginning to look hard.

"What's with me?" he said the other day. "I don't get it. I haven't been in a serious relationship in I don't know how long. It's been 4 years since I finished my coursework, and I haven't written my dissertation. Every year it's 'next year.' I don't belong to any community of people. My only hobby, if you can call it that, is bridge. I can't seem to sustain working out. Friends call, and I don't return their calls. I have terrific professional connections, and I haven't done the things I need to do to keep them up. I used to think my problem was depression or that feeling of flatness I have, but it's like I'm panning out from that and when I look at the big picture it's everywhere: this lack of connection—to myself, my work, to other people."

"I don't want to sound too New Agey, but it's as though there's a deeper self buried inside of me. I don't know whether to call it a deeper self, more spiritual, truer, creative, or more cherished self, but I do know I do not have a coherent sense of self my life flows out of. It's as though I'm a collection of experiences and events, a rolling stone gathering no moss. My life is episodic, like a picaresque novel, going from one loosely connected episode to another. Nothing sticks. I just don't get it."

I don't get it either, not really. I am awed by Ben's description of himself, how detailed, how articulate it is, what a well-drawn psychological portrait it is. It is like British psychoanalyst Harry Guntrip's (1968) portrait of a schizoid personality. It is a perfect phenomenological description. But it is not a dynamic or genetic explanation. What created this picture and what keeps it going? I asked these questions aloud, and my mind returned to what Ben told me had been his earliest memory. He was 2 years old and about to put his pacifier into his mouth. He looked down at it and wondered, "Am I too old for this?"

How does a 2 year old wonder if he is too old for a pacifier, if he is being a baby for using a pacifier? I think of Guntrip's work on the schizoid personality's early relationship to need, of such patients coming to feel ashamed of needing in their early life. Guntrip explained how when children's needs are not met they blame themselves, blame their needs, and begin to feel ashamed of themselves for having needs. And so the schizoid personality works at being self-sufficient, turning away from the humiliating experience of wanting and not receiving, of needing and not getting. How does one attach to another, perhaps even to oneself, if one does not need?

Ben has told me how he cried and got angry last summer when he visited his grandmother in a nursing home and saw the way his mother treated her now that she had had a stroke. "She infantilized her. I couldn't stand it. My grandmother dribbled water from her mouth after my mother gave her a drink and my mother wiped my grandmother's mouth and chin dry, saying, 'We can't be drooling water, now can we Mom?' I couldn't stand it," Ben said. "It was such an affront to my grandmother's dignity, the little that she had left."

Ben remembers the way his brother and sister fought when they were growing up. He has described his brother as "a pragmatic realist," the type who adopts the attitude "Get along to go along." His sister, on the other hand, was passionate and argumentative, complained, and expected things. "When they fought," Ben said, "my head was with my brother but my heart was with my sister. I was like my brother—detached, accommodating, not expecting much, intellectual. My feelings were never easy to access but I always felt they were there, underneath at a kind of primordial level. I was the only child in the family interested in literature and poetry and art. That felt like my real core, like it was nested inside of me—this aesthetic core that was feeling and sensitive, even though it was hard to access. My dad once told me that my mother felt a special connection to me that she didn't with my brother or sister around those things and that it was very important to her."

I realize now what an important moment I missed with Ben a couple of months into therapy. He was going away to a friend's wedding that weekend. When he arrived at our session that night straight from work, he was wearing a gray suit and a muted gray, brown, and ivory tie, its colors cloudlike shapes blending into one another. Ben started telling me about the wedding. He sat back in his chair as he typically did, his hands locked behind his head of curly red hair, his gaze averted to the bookcase behind me, occasionally touching base with my eyes, his voice deep and resonant. Then abruptly, as he was saying his friend had told him there would be some single women whom Ben had never met before at the wedding, he unlocked his hands from behind his head, his voice became softer, and he looked at me and said, "I was thinking I would wear this tie. What do you think?" I was stunned and, at a complete loss for what to say, said in my discomfort something like "I don't know. I'm not sure why you're asking me." I wonder what has gotten lost from that exchange and how we might regain it.

* * *

During one session Ben told me a story of his mother and her family, a story he had told me before, but this time in more detail. Ben's mother's brother died when Ben was 3 years old. Ben's grandmother had him preserved, mummified in some way, and put his body in the family mausoleum in the cemetery, where she visited him daily for years. She started drinking heavily when he died. Frequently, Ben's grandfather came home at night from work to find the older children home alone, their mother drunk and at the cemetery.

Ben stared at the wall behind me as he recalled the mausoleum from family visits there when he was a child. He remembered the gold letters engraved on the white marble boxes lining the walls like drawers. He recalled staring at the drawer that held his uncle's body, his uncle's name and dates of birth and death engraved on it. He remembered imagining the small boy lying in the box dressed in navy blue wool shorts with suspenders, a white long-sleeved shirt and navy blue tie, black knee-high socks, and patent leather oxfords—the way Ben saw his uncle dressed in a family photograph. He remembered the image that welled up in his mind of his grandmother, drunk, opening the drawer, crying, and holding her dead son to her. He could still hear a loud click, the click of the cast-iron door to the mausoleum echoing off the walls.

A terror crept into his eyes as he talked about this. "I'm in there. I'm in that mausoleum. I walk around this world bright, clever, witty, full of potential and filled with dread, the dread that I will wind up sleeping under a bridge somewhere. I've never understood why, never had the slightest inkling why that was my fantasy of myself, why everyone said I had so much potential and I saw myself as ultimately destitute, living in a cardboard box under a bridge. It's because I'm in that mausoleum, locked away, buried alive just like my uncle. I can go through the motions, no, more than that. I can get by amazingly well putting little effort into my work, my life, but in the end it isn't effort and industriousness I'm lacking. It's me. It's my very self, my real self, not the shell of myself I've been living out of. This is crazy. I hear myself talk and it sounds crazy and yet it feels so right—maybe more right than anything I've ever said in my life. That feeling self, that sensitive and aesthetic part of me always felt there, like my core, but at the same time it's barely accessible. I don't understand how or know just when it happened, but somehow it was locked away."

As I sat and listened to Ben, I saw his face change from empty to fearful to alive with a sense of the discovery he was making. Guntrip and Rank, Therese of Lisieux and Teresa of Avila, all ran through my head. Each pointed to the future, to the life force within Ben. Guntrip spoke of a deeply hidden inner heart of the self that is cut off, and Teresa of Avila said the place God dwells within is in the innermost part of the heart, and in its deepest place. Rank talked about the transcendence that is possible when one accepts the inevitability of suffering that has occurred in one's life. With acceptance, the creative will of the soul emerges, transcending the given into new life.

It feels like a sacred moment with Ben, a moment when he stands on the edge not only of understanding his past as it lives in the present but also of harnessing the transcendent, the life force, the spirit, rediscovering, bringing to light and life the deeply hidden inner heart of him lying mummified in the mausoleum.

If we are talking about Ben's soul, if we are talking about God, about the divine who dwells in Ben's innermost heart, then do we go back differently to the mausoleum than if we are going back to retrieve Ben's innermost heart of his true self, not Self? Is it different?

What does Ben mean by what he calls his spiritual self? What layers of experience are behind that? Where is this dimension in his life, and, where, if anywhere, does he want it to be? Does he see it as a force within him, a life force we can draw on and talk about, open up, and explore together?

* * *

"How do I begin?" Ben asked again at the beginning of the next session.

"I'm not sure. Should we go back to the mausoleum?"

Ben nodded and looked away, receded into himself, recalling one Sunday in his teens when he went to church and then to the cemetery with his parents. Canon Norris was giving a short talk before Sunday service on the meaning of Lent. Ben liked Canon Norris, who stood before the parishioners wearing a rumpled navy blue sport coat over his black clerical garb. He was thoughtful, musing over the question before he responded. In most rituals, including those of Lent, he said, "We enact moments of transition from the past as a key to the future." The asceticism of Lent, whether in prayer, almsgiving, or fasting, he said, is not an end in itself. Rather, we practice ascetic disciplines so that we are prepared for those moments when we will need the strength of self, equanimity, and attunement to something larger than ourselves in order to respond. He likened it to practicing backhand against a backboard. "You practice against a backboard not to mindlessly hit against a backboard, but so that you are ready in the moment a backhand comes to you in a game."

Ben knew what Canon Norris was talking about. Earlier that morning he had been hitting tennis balls against the backboard in Lincoln Park. Francis Parker, two-time winner of the U.S. Open, walked by on his way to the clubhouse. Ben watched him in awe, this tall, lean man, with his mane of silver hair. A few minutes later Frank approached Ben, explaining that his partner hadn't shown up, and asked if Ben would like to hit with him until he did.

Ben told himself to focus on his breathing, stay relaxed, and keep his eye on the ball just as he had when he'd been hitting against the backboard. Frank Parker had a beautiful stroke, but his knees had gone, so Ben would need to place the ball close to him. Frank hit with long, fluid stokes, hitting out on the ball over and over again, placing it right to Ben. Ben hit out at the ball with long, relaxed ground strokes, concentrating on staying with the ball. The two of them got into a rhythm together so that before long Ben was playing in the zone, placing shot after shot to Frank. "It was the most amazing tennis I've ever played," Ben told me. "And afterward he shook my hand, autographed one of the balls for me, and said he hoped we could hit again sometime."

After Mass, Ben and his parents drove out to the cemetery. He always hated the smell inside the mausoleum: It was dank and musty smelling, and even in the summer it seemed cold. The sunlight shone through the stained glass window over the small altar against the back wall, and the bright colors played on the white marble floor. Ben formed his hand in the shape of a beak and opened and closed it, playing with its shadow across the colors.

The drawer with his uncle's casket in it was shut like all the others'—his aunt's, his grandmother's, and his grandfather's. Ben counted the drawers—eight in all—four already filled.

"I remember hoping I would die young enough to get a drawer and be buried in the mausoleum," Ben said.

"We wouldn't have buried you in there anyhow," his mother laughed when Ben told her years later. "It's a ghost house."

Ben remembers tracing the letters of his uncle's name with his finger while his mother Windexed the windows and the glass top on the altar. He traced the name and the uncle's date of birth but stopped, as he always did, after the dash between his uncle's date of birth and date of death. He never went any further.

That Sunday a gas lawn mower started up outside, and Ben went to watch the cemetery workers on their tractor mowers. Ben's father was pulling weeds beside the mausoleum. Ben helped him until the two of them heard the sound of the cast-iron doors closing and the turning of the big iron key.

Jungian analyst Ann Ulanov (1996) states,

> Jung looks at spirit in the consulting room and looks hard ... spirit is a reality that transcends the whole psyche ... we prepare to encounter, greet, meet, and house the Self.... The Self is always there, operating on us and in us. (pp. 4, 22–23)

These were the kinds of things I was hungry to read.

* * *

Ben longed to break down. It was a fantasy, a wish, an odd idea to him, but one that recurred—that the crumbling of his defenses would be his salvation. One day as he was walking to my office he became aware of a dull feeling of sadness, and as he crossed the threshold of the door into the lobby of the building he was struck by hope, hope that something would happen that day, that this sadness in him would somehow come to a head and his defenses would break down, and in the breakdown he would arrive at a place where he could begin to come to life again. His thought was not of a fear of breakdown but a wish for a breaking down that would actually be a breakthrough.

* * *

The weekend after I asked Ben what his earliest memory was and he told me about himself holding the pacifier, he had a breakdown of sorts. He had been at a party where he had smoked some grass. "It must have been cut with something else," Ben said. "My heart started racing, then pounding so hard I thought I was going to die. The friend I had gone to the party with walked along the river with me for hours, talking me down and walking. I tried to think my way out of what was happening, telling myself I was in control, I wasn't dying, it was only the drugs, it would pass. I approximated how long it would take before it was over, speculated on what the grass might have been cut with. None of it worked. My heart kept pounding like waves crashing against the cavity of my chest, and beads of perspiration were dripping off my body. I thought I would die of a heart attack. Finally I said to myself, 'Love and trust. Those are the only things that are going to get you through this.' I started to talk to my friend about love and trust, and my heart began to slow down. For those hours, which seemed endless, love and trust were the only answers."

Ben had become aware of the soothing sound of his friend's voice, of how he kept speaking in calm, measured words telling Ben that he would be all right, that he was safe, and that the best thing to do was to give himself over to the experience, try to ride it out. Ben said he had heard the words, but, more than that, had an experience of his friend unlike any he'd had before, or could remember having, with another human being. This man, his buddy, became a palpable presence to him, a living, breathing soothing other who was right there with him in his experience, right there with him and for him. All that counted was the bond between them that very moment. That's what Ben could rely on to give him safety and reassurance he would feel. He was utterly dependent on this man to get through the nightmare he was in, and he knew he had to trust. It felt good; in the end it felt wonderful, he said, liberating, not to be relying on his thinking, his rationality. His friend and he walked up and down the promenade, and when he felt a little calmer they sat on one of the green benches by the river. "It still wasn't over," Ben said. "But it had changed. Once I surrendered it began to change. I just kept saying to myself, 'Trust,' and the pounding began to lessen."

* * *

Ben had intuited his need for his psychological defenses to break down. I had come to know the necessity for that in my life only when I had been driven to it a few years earlier. It seemed as if I was on the verge of ruining another relationship with my unrelenting fear and its offshoot of anger. Defeated and despairing, I turned to Thomas Merton's (1971) words:

> The contemplative way is the paradoxical response to the almost incomprehensible call from God drawing us into solitude, plunging us into darkness and silence, not to withdraw and protect us from peril, but to lead us through untold dangers by a miracle of love and power. (p. 92)

* * *

Over and over I read these words. I knew deeply that they were right, but I had no idea what they meant for me—not then, not beyond knowing that the only real place for me to be, the place where my innermost self was at that moment, was in the darkness and silence and that it needed the space of solitude.

I kept reading Merton. One day I came upon another passage, which said that we should let ourselves be brought "defenceless into the center of our dread [where] we stand alone before God in our nothingness, without explanations, without theories, completely dependent on God's providential care, in dire need of God's grace, God's mercy and the light of faith" (Merton, 1971, p. 69). Something clicked inside me. Analysis, thinking, processing, working at it, will, effort, determination—all of it made a difference and none of it made a difference, not ultimately. Reading these words, something in me collapsed. The only thing to do was to surrender. In surrendering to the inner dread and darkness lay the possibility of discovering the Self. I had no idea where to turn or what to do. My usual ways of being and coping were useless in the face of the fear and anger that had reflexively risen up in me in a time of hope. The only thing I knew to do was to stay close to the words of Merton and where they took me. And so I began each day spending time living in these words.

As the days went by, I came to know some of the liberation Merton speaks of near the end of his book in his quotation from *Dark Night of the Soul*:

> You would never labor so effectively ... as now, when God takes your hand and guides you in the darkness, as though you were blind, toward an end and by a way which you know not nor could you ever hope to travel with the aid of your own eyes and feet, howsoever good you may be as a walker. (1971, pp. 110–111)

* * *

It was oddly freeing to feel powerless over who I was and wanted to be. It was relieving to wait—still, quiet—in pain and fear and powerlessness. The darkness came to have its own comfort and solace, a place where I was less alone than I had been before, a place that held within it the Power and Presence I needed to find my way.

* * *

Ann Ulanov (1996) believes that "looking for and discovering the point of view of the Self ... living in the Self" (p. 13), the place where the Transcendent is felt and heard, is the ultimate goal of treatment. It is neither discovering pathology, conflict, or deficit, nor making conscious the unconscious conflicts, affects, or split-off parts of ego that are the endpoint of analysis; it is all of those but more—a supervening goal, an underlying, all-embracing goal—living in the Self. What does that mean for Ben?

* * *

"It's been a horrible couple of days," Ben said during one session. "I sat down to work on my dissertation—just to write out an outline of my thinking, of the plan of the paper—and I felt as if someone had told me I had to break my own legs. It was that painful. My ideas seemed like shit. I felt bored by them, repelled, that they had no substance."

"It's the bridge I can't do. I can stand here and look at the other side—actually being a tenured literature professor. That feels great. That feels comfortable. But it's getting from here to there that feels horrible because I don't know if I have what it takes. I don't know if my ideas have any merit or if I even have any belief, any sense of conviction, about my own ideas. I'm afraid if I delve in, if I dig for them, begin to explore them, put them down on paper they'll be awful or worse, I'll find I have no ideas, not beyond the most superficial and conventional."

"I had lunch with Larry today, my friend who just got tenure. He told me not to worry. He went through what I'm going through—thinking his ideas were horrible, seeing them on paper, and becoming completely deflated. He said it is part of the process and said I should just get my thoughts down and print them out. It made me feel a lot better."

I discussed my work with Ben in my consultation group with Alan, Debbie, Melinda, and Phil. At the end of our time, Phil said, "I keep thinking that there's an autistic quality about him—that he's like someone with Asperger's syndrome. People with Asperger's are usually very intelligent and can read social cues so they know what one ought to feel in a given situation and they simulate it, but they're not actually feeling it."

"He's pretty defended against his feelings, but he feels," I said.

"Are you sure?" Philip asked. "Stop and think back, really reflect on it. It's not so easy to detect. People with Asperger's are very good at simulating feelings, and he's so likeable it would be even harder to notice."

Time was up, and I was glad. I wanted to take Ben and pull him toward me, protect him from this talk of Asperger's. Ben doesn't have Asperger's, I thought. Ben feels.

* * *

I took my niece, who was named Therese after me, out for dinner for her birthday last night and told her about opening up *The Story of a Soul* (Therese of Lisieux, 1899/1995) and finding my father's inscription and my crayon scrawl back to him. She asked who had published the book and wondered if it was still in print.

On the way home I thought about the fact that there was another translation of Therese of Lisieux's spiritual autobiography in my bookcase next to *The Story of a Soul*. It is a larger, thicker volume, a light blue cloth-covered book entitled *The Autobiography of St. Therese*. Its imprimatur is 1958, 2 years after that of *The Story of a Soul*. I thought about someday giving it to Therese.

That night I dreamed I opened the blue-bound book, which I hadn't opened since I was a child. Throughout, text was underlined in pencil and it was filled with marginalia. At the end of one chapter, where three quarters of the page was blank, I'd written a list of single words. I was stunned to see all the underlining and notes. I had no memory of having written them, and I was glad I had not yet given the book to my niece, unaware of the treasure I had buried in it.

That morning when I awoke, I went to the bookcase and stood there a while before I picked up the book. I was hoping, wondering if I would find it as I had dreamed or if perhaps I'd find another inscription from my father—or maybe this time from my mother. But the only handwriting in it—across the inside of both the front and back covers—was a copy of a fragment of Therese's original handwritten autobiography: neat, tall, French words, evenly spaced in straight lines. I made out words and phrases here and there—God … imperfection … honor … humiliations … truth … the children … heart … humility … desire … respect. On the first page was a photograph of St. Therese in a white habit and black veil, the habit of a novice. She had a pleasant, open face—wide eyes, thin lips, a round face, a depth in her eyes.

Paging through the book, I came upon a passage where Therese talked about how she and her father used to take a walk each afternoon and make a visit to the Blessed Sacrament. Therese said that she had never had "the knack" of playing with dolls but loved to garden beside her father and had a small plot of her own, which he had given her that contained a recess on which she would put up little toy altars.

I thought of how when I was a child my father and I would walk down Longwood Drive to 7:15 a.m. Mass at St. Barnabas on weekday mornings and of sitting next to him in the front pew—the quiet, the calm, the peace of it. I remembered playing Mass at home in my bedroom with my brother Tim and sister Katie as the parishioners and brother Joe as the altar boy. We would set up the card table as the altar. I, the priest, would use my mother's sugar bowl as the ciborium. I'd tear Holsum bread into round pieces and flatten them down to make the hosts. We'd use grape juice for wine, the dinner bell for the altar bell. My youngest brother, Tom, roamed in and out of the room in his Dr. Denton's. I thought of the moment in fifth grade when boys were learning how to become altar servers and I realized with deep disappointment that I would never be able to become a priest. I thought , too, that it was that same year, when

I was in fifth grade, that my older brother Bill left to go into the Benedictine Seminary at St. Meinrad Abbey in Indiana.

I never before realized all the similarities I shared with Therese of Lisieux—or had I and I'd just forgotten?

In *The Soul's Code: In Search of Character and Calling*, Jungian analyst James Hillman (1996) said we have been robbed of our true biographies and we go into therapy to recover them. He believed we each have our own personal sense of calling, that from the beginning of our lives we have an innate individual character to which we are answerable. Hillman believed that innate image should be the central concern of every therapy and that it "does not tolerate too much straying" (p. 12).

* * *

Ben set his brown backpack on the floor and pulled out his check from it. He handed it to me with the simple word, "Sorry." I had seen his embarrassment when I opened the door, and I saw it again now in the tight set of his mouth and his gazing away at the wall. He was a month late with the check. We had been through this before and were back at it again. It was the kind of moment Ben's life was full of.

Ben had forgotten his check for weeks, then said he would send an electronic check, but didn't. Instead, he went out of town, unexpectedly canceling his appointments for that week and ignoring my call telling him that I expected the check by the end of the week. As we talked about what had transpired, Ben's face looked as if he were filling with self-loathing. I asked him about it, and he said yes, he was filling with self-loathing.

"Maybe that's the point," I said.

"The self-loathing?"

"Yeah—across all the instances in your life we've talked about where you don't follow through, miss appointments, don't finish things on time, don't return phone calls you should—across all of them the state you wind up in is one of self-loathing. It isn't really a satisfactory hypothesis, but it's a place to start, to play with together and see where it goes—maybe the point of all these things you mess up on is to keep yourself in a state of self-loathing and self-punishment."

"I think it's more like this," Ben answered. "I imagine a small child whom everyone tells, 'You can be anything.' People are always saying this to him, but all he feels inside is scared. He doesn't feel like he can be anything. He just feels scared when people say that to him."

"What is he scared of?"

"I have no idea, and neither does he. He just knows he's scared."

"What does he do with the fact that people keep telling him he could be anything he wants to be?"

"Well, they've pretty much stopped saying it now."

"Who used to say it?"

"People of his parents' generation, his parents' friends, teachers, sometimes even his peers. But when they say it he gets an image of himself as a small child looking up at a big world where everyone is taller and bigger, and buildings are huge and towering, and he's too small to be out there in that world being anything."

"How does a parent communicate to a child that when he grows up he's going to be someone?" Ben wondered aloud. "I seemed to float through life, never sure of who I was or who I was going to become. I used to get by with minimal effort. I did a lot of things well, mostly academics, and wasn't required to do anything I didn't want to do. I quit Boy Scouts. I quit violin. I signed up to go away to camp, but then decided at the last minute I didn't want to go and my parents said fine. I got into Yale but went to Princeton. My parents and brothers were college professors. I went to grad school pretty reflexively. But now things are arcing downward. My cohorts got teaching jobs 3 years ago. I haven't written my dissertation, and I'm teaching at a community college on a year-to-year basis."

* * *

Just a few days earlier, when Ben's father drove him to the airport to return to New York, he had wished him a happy New Year and said, "The most important thing is to be healthy, but try to become happy, too."

"He didn't say, 'Be happy.' He said, 'Try to become happy.'" Ben's eyes misted up. I asked him what he was feeling.

"Sad. There's my 80-year-old father telling his son to try to become happy."

"That is sad," I said, my eyes misting up too.

"He and my mom have to suck all the enjoyment they can out of my older sister and her family."

It was time for the session to end. I said, "You know, your hope right now is in your sadness. It's in your staying connected to your feeling sad."

"I know. That's why I'm going now to see a sad movie. It seems like the right thing to do."

Ben left his backpack behind as he walked to the door. "You've left your backpack," I told him.

* * *

On one of our first warm and sunny spring days, I opened my living room window as wide as it would go and sat at my writing table overlooking the East River and the Triborough Bridge. I sat, trying to write, the white noise of traffic from FDR Drive and the calls of children on the playground across the street in the background. I thought about Ben and what he needed from me and recalled something my father had once said.

When my father first started losing his memory, the psychiatrist he was seeing sent him for a neuropsychological evaluation. The psychiatrist and I talked on the phone after he received the results.

"It's a form of dementia, but I don't think it's Alzheimer's," he said. "The pattern is too atypical."

After we finished talking about the results, he said, "Your father's an amazing man, an amazing man," and he went on to say how my father had such psychic strength, how successfully he had lived his life even with all its early brokenness. "An amazing man," he said again in his Austrian accent as we were hanging up.

That weekend my parents came to dinner.

We talked about the test results, all relieved the diagnosis wasn't Alzheimer's, although still worried about where this memory loss was going. Then I said to my dad, "Dr. Gruness really loves you, Dad."

"That's the therapy," he said.

I thought about how individual it was with each patient—whether and how love entered a therapy—and said, "But it doesn't always work out that way, Dad."

He shrugged and said, "Still, that's the therapy."

* * *

It was Holy Thursday evening. "Stay here and wait with me. Wait and pray," Jesus said to the apostles in the Garden of Gethsemane. His "soul sorrowful to the point of death," he went and knelt by a rock and prayed. When he came back the apostles had fallen asleep, Luke says from sheer grief.

Ben arrived in tennis shoes and a rumpled, spotted beige crewneck sweater. He said he was tired and his brain was fuzzy. "At least I don't think that means I have a brain tumor, or at least not necessarily, like I thought last fall."

Ben, asleep on his own anguish, the sharp edge of it dulled by years of pushing away from himself and others, was left in a chronic state of grayness punctuated by a vague sadness. The goal was to help him awaken to his anguish and, regardless of how painful it was, not to fall asleep or otherwise look away, but to stay awake with him.

Ben said, "I don't know. Sometimes I think my whole problem is a problem of connection. I wonder if they have any medication for that. I can hear the television commercials now, the voice-over saying, 'If you have problems connecting with yourself and other people and this symptom has persisted more than a week, ask your doctor about ...'"

I laughed and Ben stiffened a bit. He went on, "When I was little I was fascinated by those refrigerator magnets. I used to play with them all the time. You know the ones that head toward each other, then veer off at the last moment as they're about to connect? That's how I think of myself sometimes, that whatever the physics of that is it's the physics of my psyche also. I start to head toward myself and then at the last moment veer off and never make the connection. Sometimes I think there's nothing inside to connect with. I'd rather not know, so I stay in a state of unknowing and disconnection rather than find out. I think of being in a relationship and I worry that the other person will literally see right through me—because there really is nothing inside of me."

"When I do get in a relationship, I feel this suppressed but powerful urge to merge. It is a wish to have absolutely no barriers, to be completely transparent, and pour out everything that is inside of me and be fully understood. And then I find myself making some invidious comparison or retreating into silence and lethargy or making a sarcastic remark."

"Do you feel fear between the wish and pushing away?" I asked.

"No. It's like it's on automatic pilot. One follows the other without my really being aware of it until I look back and reflect. So that's about it. That's all I know."

This was such a frequent point to come to with Ben—first to the point of a very astute phenomenological description and then a wall, no digging deeper, getting under. There was nothing he seemed to grab on to or that seemed to take hold inside him to push him further and take him deeper. We waited together in this frustrating place, waiting for something new to move, to emerge from within the gates of the garden.

* * *

"Maybe I should face the fact that I'll never complete my dissertation and become a high school English teacher," Ben said one day. "I'd be disappointed, but I'd get used to it. It would be a relief as well as a disappointment. My parents would be disappointed, and they wouldn't be able to brag about me to their friends like they could about me, but, as my dad said to me over the holidays, my happiness is the most important thing. Maybe I need to accept the fact I don't want to be a college professor."

"All those computer games I play, the amount of bridge I play—they feel like they're screening something out. You know, like on the subway when the sound system has feedback and the noise is so piercing. I turn my Walkman on so I won't hear the screeching but as the song is coming to an end I start thinking about the screeching, bracing myself for it to be there in the pause between songs. That's what the way I spend my life feels like—I divert my attention and energy into these meaningless, adolescent activities to block out some noise that lies behind it."

* * *

"How do I get to it? How do I get to this deeper self?" Ben asked at the beginning of another session. "The problem is, when I am in my intellectual self the tie to this better self is so thin I don't have the desire to go over into this other self. I don't know how to access it."

"I'm thinking," I said, "that maybe one way to begin to access it here is to just think back to when you first felt it. Think of when and where and how in your childhood you knew this self. Go as far back as you can remember, and then move forward in time. Or, think about those moments in your life now when you even get glimmers of this self."

Ben sat back and stretched out his arms behind his head in his habitual pose, looking toward the ceiling, thinking. He was wearing a green turtleneck and had gotten a haircut, which made him look a little younger.

"In my adolescence I became aware of a duality in me. I remember thinking about it when I was 14. I recall trying to talk to my parents about it and thinking they didn't understand. When I was 13 I'd learned some basic computer programming and set up a little class in my basement and taught other kids in the neighborhood, and I remember clearly thinking I didn't want to do that anymore—that I could be a computer geek, but if I was, I'd be turning away from this other side of myself. In part, my awareness of this more cherished self came about through my discovering relationships. It was the time I started kissing girls and developing some friendships with other boys. I wasn't content to just play anymore. Most of my play as a child had been solitary. I remember I used to say as a teenager, 'At 13, I discovered computers, and, at 14, I discovered relationships.' Certain books and music made me feel this other part of myself, this deeper, better part, a spiritual part of me in the loose sense of that word. It was around that time I became aware of feelings. I remember going to the movies with a bunch of other kids and afterwards, when we were talking about the movie the other kids talked so much about what feelings were evoked in them by the movie and I hardly had any feelings. I went home and said to my dad that other kids seemed to have more feelings than I did or more access to their feelings. My dad said he knew what I meant. He told me he felt that way himself sometimes, too, but then he said, 'Don't worry about it. Half the time people say they're having feelings, I think they're faking it.' I don't know. Maybe I was aware of this duality even when I was younger—like maybe even when I was 2 wondering if I was too old for a pacifier or when I was 7 years old and decided I wanted to show that I was liberal and sensitive and so I invited all girls to my birthday party and just one other boy. That was the age when it was like girls had cooties. Only I wasn't liberal and sensitive. I sat in the corner of the room with the other boy talking to him the whole time."

"It seems like the times when this side of me comes out most is in a crisis. I have fantasies of being with a woman and falling apart and all of this feeling flooding out of me, with her understanding and accepting and loving me with all my feelings. The time I had the bad drug trip was the time this side of me most emerged and saved my life."

"But that was a crisis. On a day-to-day basis the most I do is throw a sop to my deeper self by turning away from things that will inexorably lead me away from it, like becoming a computer geek, but I don't do the work of that better self, like figure out how to have relationships and really do the hard work of it. When people say to me you can be anything you want to be, maybe I get terrified because they're speaking about the intelligent, detached, analytical self. They don't even see this deeper, better self—how could they? I barely see it myself."

Listening to Ben, I thought of Teresa of Avila speaking about the first mansion in the interior castle, the mansion of self-knowledge. She said,

The soul should not remain for a long time in one single room—not, at least, unless it is in the room of self-knowledge. How necessary that is…. However high a state the soul may have attained, self-knowledge is incumbent upon it. (1577/1961, p. 37)

And then, "It is no small pity and should cause us no little shame that, through our own fault, we do not understand ourselves, or know who we are." She continued, "Although this is only the first Mansion, it contains riches of great price" (p. 29).

Ben continued, "There's a part of me that's in limbo and doesn't want to emerge or is out of focus and doesn't want to come into focus and become integrated into the rest of me. It feels like it's not ready to."

"What does it need to be ready? What's the first thing that comes to mind?" I asked.

Ben thought for a moment. "It needs someone to patiently allow it to grow into itself," he answered.

"What would that look like?"

"I have no idea."

"See if you can see. Let an image come to you."

"I see an image of me lying in bed, the whole issue of work is completely set aside, and I'm lying in bed with someone sitting next to me while I'm healing. Actually, it's probably just my laziness—that's why I'm lying there in bed like a slouch."

"I don't think so. I think the image is telling you what you need."

"I need some kind of plan, some goal-oriented plan."

"There isn't a plan for your deepest self to grow. The image is telling you where you need to begin. Let it unfold."

"Did I tell you my father called and suggested he and I go away for a couple of days, just the two of us together?"

"No, you didn't."

"Yeah. I called him last week to talk with him about how stuck I feel, how I don't know if I'm going to be able to get it together to write my dissertation or if I even want to try to. Yesterday he called and said maybe it would be good if he and I spent some time together."

"That's really lovely."

"Yeah. It is," Ben said, his face moist with tears. "And my mom is really being gracious about it. I'm sure it's hard for her to be left out."

"Your association just gave you the next step—to go and be with your father."

"I'd really like that," Ben said, crying harder.

* * *

"Just as I walked into the building today I felt sad," Ben said as he sat down. "I don't know what it was, but in some way it felt like it could be a beginning—either good or bad, like I might have some kind of breakthrough here today and things would start coming together—or it might be the beginning of things unraveling. There was a feeling of relief that went with it—like even if it's the beginning of my life unraveling, at last it's a beginning."

"What is your thought about your life unraveling?" I asked him.

"I've had that thought for years. I remember in college thinking about the trajectory of my life and imagining I'd graduate and go to grad school and, after that, start my career teaching, but that in the end I'd wind up sleeping under a bridge. Like in the 80s when we had the quote 'homelessness' problem, before we got 'compassion fatigue,' that I'd end up one of those guys with a Ph.D. sleeping in a cardboard box. I don't know. I don't know where this sadness comes from. Maybe it's the weather."

It was in the 40s that day, raining off and on. Ben went on to tell me about a story he'd read in the *New Yorker* that morning; he thought that maybe that's what had brought on this funk.

"I took a writing class during graduate school," Ben said. "I was terrible and I was so shocked. I'd never been terrible at anything verbal in my life. The way the class ran, when it was time for your piece to be critiqued you brought your story in and read it out loud to everyone. That's what I imagined doing this morning. I imagined myself sitting in the class reading this great story to my classmates and them sitting there in rapt attention. That's what I always do when I read stories—ever since I took that class. And this morning as I was doing that I wondered if there was a place inside me I could go to write that kind of story."

"Your sadness this morning."

"No."

"Why?"

"I can't go there."

"Why not?"

"I can't. I just don't do that. That's not who I am."

"That's why you couldn't write. People write out of their own core emotions."

"I know."

"It's as if you've never grabbed hold of yourself."

"That's exactly right."

"And the surest way to begin to do that right now is to grab hold of the sadness you came in here feeling. You grab hold of that and then you grab hold of the next experience inside of you and the next and gradually you begin to feel like you have a self that coheres and that you're living out of."

"I've always been afraid there's nothing there."

"What was the story in the *New Yorker* about that you read this morning?"

Taking off his glasses and staring at the bookcase on the back wall of my office, Ben told me, "It's about death and what dies with someone and what lives on when someone dies. In the story there is a woman who dies leaving a piece of amber in the bottom drawer of her dresser. It got me thinking about what would live on if I died—and in whom. There's no one who would know what was in my dresser drawer. I asked Larry at lunch if his wife would know what was in his bottom dresser drawer if he died. He laughed and said, 'You've got to be kidding.' I told him I was dead serious. I wanted to know if his wife would know."

"He finally said, 'Yeah. She knows. Does it matter?'"

"Sure it does," I said.

"'How in God's name could it possibly matter?' Larry asked me, and then he doubled over laughing. The people at the table behind us all turned around to see what was so funny. When he sat up and saw my face, he said, 'I'm sorry. I don't understand how in the world it matters.'"

"'You would if you didn't have a wife who knew,' I told him."

* * *

The other day I awoke to the painful sense of longing I have been feeling lately. It was right there, filling my chest as soon as I awoke. It is a feeling of longing that recurs with some regularity in my life. I have a rich life. I have wonderful friends and family. I also live quite a solitary life, and there are moments and stretches of time when I feel acutely alone and filled with unsatisfied yearning and its attendant grief. A wedding, birth, or graduation in the lives of my family and friends' families can set this longing into motion. At this point in my life, it mostly takes the form of longing for the deep knowing and being known, the unspoken comfort that comes after years of intimacy and the joyful pride of experiencing one's own children emerge into adulthood and have children of their own.

Waking to this feeling, I reached over to my nightstand for Teresa of Avila (1577/1961) and opened to this passage:

> I think that all trials would be well endured if they led to the enjoyment of these gentle yet penetrating touches of God's love. This, sisters, you will have experienced for I think that when the soul reaches the Prayer of Union, God begins to exercise this care over us ... when this experience comes to you remember that it belongs to this innermost mansion, where God dwells in our souls. (p. 222)

* * *

I lay there feeling the pain in my body, a kind of grieving and longing mixed into one, feeling overcome by and weary of it. I reread Teresa's words and sank down into them, letting them take me to that place that is both below and beyond—the place that holds the pain, opening to the peace, the stillness that surrounds then permeates the pain, not erasing it, but transforming it, that irreducible state of being in which there is strength and courage, love and compassion, peace, the pain now happening inside of this state, the state of grace, the state of God. I think that God is a state of being that both is within us and transcends us, a state of being that is open to us to participate in at every moment.

* * *

"I have this wish," Ben said, "that I will get into a relationship and it will knock what I need into me—enthusiasm, energy, curiosity, creativity, imagination, love. I know it's irrational, but it's a wish, a hope, really, that I carry. I don't see how else it will happen. It's certainly not happening from within me."

As Ben went on, I half listened and half turned over in my mind what he had just said. I thought about Guntrip's (1968) ideas about how the deeper self is first born in the relationship, how it is in relationships that one first finds oneself, and it is the relationship that heals in therapy. And I wondered how far off Ben was.

I interrupted him. "Are those qualities you wish to have knocked into you by a relationship feelings you experience in yourself when you are with your parents or ever did?"

Ben looked taken aback, then said, "What an interesting question." After considering it, he said, "No, not really. There aren't bad things that I feel when I'm with my parents. But those other qualities aren't there either."

"It's more of an absence," I suggested.

"Right," he said.

"What I'm thinking about is about the truth your fantasy contains, the possibility. It's not simply a wild, unrealistic fantasy. The grain of truth in it is that those internal experiences you name do come about in relationships. You don't autistically go off in a room alone and feel energy, enthusiasm, creativity, curiosity, love. Those are feelings that come about with other people to a large extent."

"So what do I do now? I can't go back and get that experience now."

"You can't go back and get it, but you might be able to get it now—in relationship to people in your life now, perhaps even with your parents."

I was thinking about our relationship—wondering if Ben could consider finding those qualities in himself in and through the relationship he has with me. I held back from saying anything about it. I might have been wrong, but I didn't think just then that he could acknowledge that as a possibility. I didn't want to risk his sarcasm. Then, too, the intimacy of the need felt frightening.

* * *

Freud (1915) wrote,

> The treatment must be carried out in abstinence.... I shall state it as a fundamental principle that the patient's need and longing should be allowed to persist in her, in order that they may serve as forces impelling her to do work and make changes, and that we must beware of appeasing those forces by means of surrogates. (p. 165)

Ben's first analysis was a classical one. "I could do it standing on my head," Ben told me. "I'm good at being deprived. I was one of the last Dr. Spock babies. He was out of fashion by the time I was born, but my parents believed in him. I'll never forget the first time I asked my analyst a question. He didn't answer it. He sat silently behind the couch. I distinctly remember thinking, 'Okay. Fine. I know how to do this.' And I never again asked him another question. A year or so into my treatment, a friend asked, 'Do you have a relationship with your analyst? Is that a part of how it works?' 'No, he's like a Pez dispenser,' I told him. 'I free associate and every once in a while, usually just at the end of the session, he gives an interpretation of what I've been saying.'"

Classical analyses are not for people who have been emotionally deprived or distanced. They have "been there and done that," as Ben put it. What disturbs such people is closeness. When I come close to Ben I can see his equilibrium going; that's when he brushes me away with a subtle critical or superior remark and I have to call on the wisdom of Guntrip (1968): "There are, of course, times when the only therapeutic way of relating is not to relate, when the patient would feel smothered or overwhelmed or swallowed up.... In a relationship, one must know how to wait" (p. 185).

The danger is that the waiting will slide into a passive acceptance of the status quo, a futile waiting, and eventually a stalemate, rather than an active waiting in which the dialectical tension of growth the patient is caught in finds its way—the tension between the fact that a solid and real sense of self and one's individuality can be discovered and grow only in a secure relationship, but the nascent self feels easily overwhelmed and lost in closeness with another. The hope is to discover the uniqueness that is Ben's, name it, and cultivate it, so that it can emerge and guide his unfolding development. It means I need to stay aware of the paradox that his capacity to use my support depends on his strength of self, but that his strength of self can develop only with my support— sometimes like walking a tightrope.

* * *

It was noon. The Angelus was ringing from Grace Episcopal Church across the street. Ben was late. I sat in the window seat in my office, looking out across the street at the rose window of the church and at the buds that had begun to appear on the magnolia tree in the churchyard. Work was being done on the church, and the scaffolding climbed the bell tower, a transparent orange shroud covering it. At the bottom of the scaffolding, just above the entrance to the church, a billboard had been put up. On it was an ad from Citibank that read, "If you think cutting your own hair is a good way to save money, it's not." I chuckled, then thought of the words I had read that morning that Thomas Merton (1993) wrote to a friend—"Like everyone else in the world you are almost too shy about your religious possibilities" (p. 13)—and imagined them on the billboard instead.

* * *

The buzzer rang. Ben looked relaxed as he walked in. There was almost a spring in his step.

"Some of that truer self is coming back. I don't know how it's happening and it's hard to explain, but just before coming here I picked up the phone and called four friends and left messages for them. I had lunch yesterday with Larry, and he did this strict bit which actually seemed funny to me. I didn't feel like I was just going along with it and laughing."

Ben was in a rumpled black cotton turtleneck and unpressed khakis. "I'm slumming," he said. "I don't have to teach today. I'm concerned. I'm losing my connection to my work. It's like the pilot light is going out. I worked on Saturday, read a couple of articles, and I should have done more but after a couple of hours it was as though all my energy had been drained out of me. What I need to be doing at this point is seriously challenging my ideas, really submitting them to my own tough questioning, seeing how they stand up. But I don't seem to be able to summon up the energy for it. I can't get engaged with what I'm reading and thinking about. It feels like I can't connect to the ideas."

I thought of Ben with me—how he didn't engage, connect, how when I reached out to engage him, to connect with him emotionally, he brushed me away and stepped back all at once. I thought of his description of his previous treatment and how he was surprised at how alive and communicative he has been with me. With his former therapist he said he spent many sessions feeling bogged down, flat, and detached.

I asked him if he was aware that when I reached out to engage him emotionally, he brushed me off and took a step back. "Sometimes," he said. "I'm probably at least half aware of it sometimes. I'm sure there are times I do it I'm completely unaware of it."

"I'm wondering if we looked at those moments between us when they occur whether it would give you some insight into what happens to you with your work. The problem you have with your work is the same problem you have in relationships—the problem of sustaining an alive connection, really engaging and being engaged by the other."

"Yeah," he said. "It would probably be easier to see it here as it's happening rather than at home when I'm trying to work. Its source is so layered over. It's like a castle with moats around it and walls upon walls and cul-de-sacs. Whatever it's about is highly defended and fortified at this point—from myself getting at it or anyone else."

Ben talked about his feeling of spiritual deadness. I asked him what spirituality meant in his life and what it had meant for him historically. He said he was using the term in its broadest sense—not in the religious sense of relating to a personal deity but in the sense of an animating spirit within. But, then again, sometimes he fears that's only wishful thinking, that perhaps this idea of a spirit or core residing within is a fiction, an illusion that keeps him from knowing the utter emptiness that comprises the core of him.

Ben remembered a dream. In the dream he was walking in the dark. It was pitch black. He couldn't see anything. He was on a gravel road. He had the distinct impression he was in a town and there were buildings and houses set back from the road. The sky began to lighten, not enough that he could see his surroundings but it wouldn't be long. He started to worry about it getting lighter. And then, as it was on the verge of happening, he filled with fear that he might find himself in the midst of an endless, empty expanse.

I wondered about this catastrophic inner emptiness he feared—what it was about, where it came from, whether there was a fear behind the fear. I was about to pose these questions out loud, but glanced at the clock.

"Looks like we have to stop," Ben said. I said we did.

"So maybe we can start looking at those moments of the brush-off and the step back," Ben said as he got up.

"Sure," I said.

As I opened the door for him, he walked by me with his head down and half turned away, the way he usually left, but there was a half smile on his face.

After Ben left I sat in the window seat for a while looking out at the churchyard, watching the massive willow tree swaying in the breeze. It was one of the first warm days in the city. The sun was shining brightly, and there were already a few people walking down the street using their umbrellas as parasols. I thought back over the session with Ben and to his image of a castle so fortified that he could not get inside. It reminded me of Teresa of Avila (1577/1961) remarking that many people spend much of their lives outside the walls of the castle. She wrote, "As to what good qualities there may be in our souls or Who dwells within them or how precious they are—those are things which we seldom consider and so we trouble little about the soul's beauty" (p. 29).

Ben had gone to the shore with his father for the weekend. He talked to him about the idea he had for his dissertation and, in the course of talking, conceptualized the dissertation in such a clear and cogent way he felt he could see it as a whole, knew where it was going, and what he needed to do.

"This is a perilous time, though," he said. "There's a pressure to not knowing, a pressure to keep working. Now I know I've got it. It's going to happen. I can do this. And now is when I might sit back—because I know that I can do it. But I can't do that. I've got to write this, and when it's over and I've got a teaching position I've got to keep writing. I can't be one of those people who gets on a faculty, gets tenure, then sits back and doesn't write another thing and all their colleagues hold them in contempt. This is my life."

"How does that feel to say, 'This is my life'?"

Ben thought a moment. "It doesn't feel real. I know it's real. But it doesn't feel real."

"Like you're disconnected from it?" I asked him.

"Yeah."

"Can you shift your mind from thinking analytically, rationally, and see if there's an image there about what this looks like, an image of yourself disconnected from the conviction 'This is my life'?"

"It's somewhat like the image of me dawdling on the way to school."

"Tell me about that again. I see you walking up a hill. Is that right?"

"Yes. The school was on a hill. I would be walking along, dawdling on the way to school, realizing I could be late. It was like creating a space for myself between the constraints of school and the constraints of home—not that either of them was hellacious. I had a good old time in both places. But it was like it was an act of freedom—only freedom by denial, the freedom of saying no. It wasn't an individuating act, an act of real freedom—like I was missing school because I was going to practice my ice skating to become better at it."

"How old were you?"

"Eleven or 12. I can see myself walking down the street. I'd be dawdling and realize I was going to be late, then speed up, then find myself dawdling again and speed up again. Then one day as I was dawdling and about to speed up I realized, 'I could just be late.' It was almost an erotic sensation, like ah-h-h-h-h—and that's when I became chronically late for school, just a minute or so, not enough to cause a big scene but enough to be late."

* * *

There was something about Ben's tie that caught my eye. I found my glance falling on it as he talked. He looked more handsome, younger, maybe thinner today. I wondered if he had gotten a haircut. I couldn't tell for sure, or maybe he was back on his diet and losing some weight. He wasn't wearing glasses—but wait, did he usually wear glasses? How could I not know? No—it was just that there was something different about his eyes—they looked clearer, a little more alive than usual. But the tie, something about the tie kept pulling my eye back to it. "Was that the tie Ben had thought about wearing to the wedding?" I wondered.

"No one is home. Not in my life," he was saying. "It's as though it runs on automatic pilot. And who would ever understand the way I am? I know I ask questions like this a lot, but am I the only one in the world who is like this?"

"No. You're not," I said.

"Well, I certainly don't know anyone else who is. You seem to really have a grasp of what my life is like, but that's because I pay you to sit and listen to me blab on and on."

Ben started to say more. I interrupted him.

"What if the reason I understand what your life is like is not because you pay me to listen to you blab on and on, but because what you're talking about is human—the depth and magnitude of it may be different from others, but what you're talking about is human, and maybe because of that I know it from the inside out?"

"Well, I just don't think there are many people who live such passionless lives as I. Six, 10 years ago in therapy I used to describe the problem as being that I just didn't get excited about things but I see now it's much deeper than that."

"How did you feel when I said maybe I understand not because you pay me to but because I understand what you're saying from the inside out?"

"I wanted to retreat, pull back."

"Why?"

"I feel ashamed. I don't want you to know me from the inside out. It's bad enough you see the outside, how pathetic my life is. I don't want you to also see what's deep inside me, know me from the inside out."

"What I meant was that I know what you're experiencing from the inside out because being afraid, feeling ashamed, not living out of a deeper self is a human problem, a common, if not a universal, problem to one extent or another. I know it in you because of its resonance in me, because I can feel my way into what you're saying out of my own experience."

Ben stopped. He looked surprised and his mouth hung open, momentarily speechless.

"I don't know. I don't know how I feel about that," he said, laughing. "Hmm. This is actually very funny," he said, laughing louder and shaking his head. "You're saying you're connecting to me as another human being."

"Right."

"And all this time I've been telling you how I have this longing to be utterly transparent with another human being, to have someone see everything about me and accept and love me. But here you tell me you understand me because you connect to me through your own experience as another human being and I want to run away. It makes no sense."

"You live in an emotional triangle of longing and fear and shame, moving back and forth among them."

"So other people have this problem too? This is something that is known, recognized as a syndrome or whatever that some people have?"

"Right."

"So why aren't there any 12-step programs for it? Why isn't there a place you can go to get over it? I mean, aren't there some exercises I can do?"

"We're doing what you can do. We're doing it as we speak."

"But aren't there some remedies, some life remedies, or whatever? Like get a dog, learn how to take care of it, let it depend on you, depend on it—exercises in life like that?" he said, laughing at his own proposal.

I laughed, too, and said, "That couldn't hurt."

"But seriously," he said, "suppose the antidote is something like, just as a category to sum up a variety of things that are probably needed, love. Suppose that getting through the fear and shame of being exposed and seen to be nothing but a fat, hairy slob, getting through that to finding—and I'm not sure how much of it is finding and how much of it is creating this deeper, truer self—this self where there is passion and life—if what is needed is this category of responses called love from another human being but you're not ready to be loved—it's too scary and too exposing—then where does that leave me?"

"One place that leaves you is right here," I said slowly and deliberately. "Right here."

4 Ferenczi and the Case of Matt*

I sit in the window seat of my office reflecting before heading home. It's a muggy summer day with a bit of a breeze coming through the window. The church bells are ringing that it is 7:00. Down below and across the street a young couple, both wearing backpacks, approaches the black wrought iron doors of Grace Episcopal Church. The man pushes then pulls on the door handles. The church is locked.

My mind wanders to Sándor Ferenczi, the psychoanalyst I teach a course on at the New York University Postdoctoral Program in Psychotherapy and Psychoanalysis, and to how he was locked out of the psychoanalytic community at the time of his death in 1933 and for many years later. His writings suppressed by the psychoanalytic community, his ideas discredited, and his reputation slandered, Ferenczi was rarely heard from again in the psychoanalytic world until the late 1980s.

Believing contemporary psychoanalysis would be receptive to Ferenczi, French psychoanalyst Judith Dupont arranged to have the clinical diary that Ferenczi kept toward the end of his life translated from its original German, first into French in 1985 and then into English in 1989. At the same time, a new group of psychoanalysts was emerging in the United States, called relational psychoanalysts. With

---

*This chapter originally appeared in *Contemporary Psychoanalysis*, 44(4), 2008. Reprinted with permission.

some coming from the Freudian track and others from the interpersonalist track at New York University's Postdoctoral Program in Psychotherapy and Psychoanalysis, these analysts held in common both ideas and a sensibility that resonated deeply with what Ferenczi had promoted decades earlier. A synergy developed between Ferenczi and the new relational analysts, catalyzing fresh, creative thinking in psychoanalysis that has had profound implications for the practice of psychoanalytic treatment. In retrospect, these words of Ferenczi (1929) proved to be prophetic:

> The sudden emergence in modern psychoanalysis of portions of an earlier technique and theory should not dismay us; it merely reminds us that, so far, no single advance has been made in analysis which has had to be entirely discarded as useless, and that we must constantly be prepared to find new veins of gold in temporarily abandoned workings. (p. 120)

* * *

It is 1908, and Sigmund Freud and Sándor Ferenczi are having tea in the parlor of Freud's home in Vienna. This is the first time Ferenczi, age 35, and Freud, age 52, have met. Ferenczi's face is brimming with excitement and admiration. As they talk on, Freud becomes more and more intent. Although Ferenczi, a neurologist, has read Freud's work, this meeting marks the beginning of his lifelong dedication to the field of psychoanalysis. Freud is so taken with Ferenczi that he invites him to present a paper at the first psychoanalytical congress in Salzburg that spring and to join the Freud family on holiday that summer. Ferenczi and Freud were to grow close over the years, vacationing together, travelling between Vienna and Budapest to visit each other, collaborating in their work, and developing a close friendship. Ferenczi asks Freud to analyze him, and initially Freud resists. In the face of Ferenczi's persistence, however, Freud's reluctance eventually gives way. Between 1914 and 1916, Ferenczi travels from Budapest to Vienna for three short periods of psychoanalysis with Freud, totaling 7 weeks. This is Ferenczi's only formal analysis.

Freud had had other favored disciples over the years, including Carl Jung, Alfred Adler, and Otto Rank. Their relationship with Freud could not sustain the tension when their thinking diverged too strongly from Freud's. Each of these relationships had ended in a bitter rupture with Freud. All of these men were ostracized from the psychoanalytic establishment, and their mental health maligned within the psychoanalytic community on the basis of their "extreme" thinking.

For the time being, Ferenczi and Freud's relationship flourishes. In 1919 Ferenczi (in Dupont, 1994) writes of how dependent he has grown to be on Freud: "It seems that I am only able to enjoy life and work, when I can be, and can stay on good terms with you" (p. 312).

Concerned about a growing divide in the field between psychoanalytic theory and practice, Freud proposes a competition for the best paper integrating theory and clinical technique. Ferenczi and Rank begin writing a joint paper, then they feel they can't do justice to their subject in a paper and withdraw from the competition, instead writing the book *The Development of Psychoanalysis* (1924). It is with this paper that significant tension between Freud and Ferenczi begins. They write back and forth to each other, coming to terms with the fact that they disagree. Their disagreements widen and deepen as Ferenczi increasingly pursues his own independent thinking. The tension comes to a head at the annual meeting of the International Congress of Psychoanalysis in Wiesbaden in 1931. Prior to the meeting, Ferenczi reads the paper he plans to present to Freud, "The Confusion of Tongues" (1933), in which he challenges Freud's thinking that patient reports of sexual molestation as children are largely based on fantasy. Freud implores Ferenczi not to proceed with presenting his paper, but Ferenczi goes ahead. From this point on, until Ferenczi's early death in 1933, their relationship is riddled with conflict, disappointment, and anger. Both men struggle to maintain their friendship and do remain in contact until Ferenczi's death, but the relationship always seems to be breathing its last breath.

In 1931 Freud (in Dupont, 1994) writes Ferenczi,

At last, again a sign of life and love from you! After so long time! No doubt ... you move more and more far away from me ... I am not responsible for that ... there is nobody, even in recent times, whom I would prefer to you. (p. 314)

And a few months later he writes, "At least I did my best faithfully to play my father-role. Now, follow your own way." (p. 314)

In 1932, Ferenczi contracts pernicious anemia, a blood disease. He attributes his physical illness to his emotional reaction to the rift with Freud:

> The blood crisis arose when I realized that not only can I not rely on the protection of a "higher power" [Freud] but on the contrary I shall be trampled under foot by this indifferent power as soon as I go my own way and not his. (p. 316)

Each man feels abandoned and betrayed by the other. Yet, near the end of Ferenczi's life in 1933, Freud's affection for his friend and former patient shows through. Freud (1933) writes in his final letter to Ferenczi before Ferenczi's death,

> I ask you, let all the hard work rest for now; your handwriting really shows how tired you still are. The discussions about your technical and theoretical innovations can wait, and will only profit from lying fallow. It is more important to me for you to regain your health. (pp. 448–449)

Ferenczi was not to regain his health, dying within weeks of receiving this last letter.

His fate in the psychoanalytic community is much the same as that of those who were closest to Freud before him. His later writings go unpublished, and it is widely rumored they are the product of a mind gone mad, though those who had been in personal contact with Ferenczi during this time resolutely dispute this.

* * *

Ferenczi's *Clinical Diary* (1932/1988), a project on which he was working at the time of his death, went unpublished until 1985. The *Clinical Diary* is a record Ferenczi kept of his clinical work and experimentation in 1932. In the words of its editor, Judith DuPont, it is "a history of the multiple transferences and countertransferences that intertwine in an analytic practice, reported with unusual candor" (p. xxvi).

In a letter to Freud, Ferenczi (1932/1988) described what the purpose of writing the *Clinical Diary* was about for him:

> It seems that I would like to recuperate now from half a lifetime of super-performances. By 'rest' I mean here immersing myself

in a kind of scientific 'poetry and truth' from which one day, perhaps—at times I believe definitely—something not without value will emerge. (1932/1988, p. xvi)

Ferenczi opened himself to the reader in the *Clinical Diary*. He struggles with and for his patients, works tirelessly, and oscillates between excitement and despair about the innovations he was experimenting with in psychoanalysis. He was deeply moved by his patients and unusually open to their reactions to him. He analyzed patients whom others had designated untreatable, gaining him the reputation of "the analyst of last resort." The *Clinical Diary* is a testimony to a change that was occurring in Ferenczi. Throughout it, he wrestles with his own self-critique: "Instead of feeling with the heart, I feel with my head" (1932/1988, p. 86).

In the diary, Ferenczi urges psychoanalysts to use their method of treatment with more elasticity and creativity, which often means becoming more actively engaged in the treatment. Ferenczi (1932/1988) himself gives us an example of this:

Patients cannot believe that an event really took place, or cannot fully believe it, if the analyst, as the sole witness of the events, persists in his cool, unemotional, and, as patients are fond of stating, purely intellectual attitude, while the events are of a kind that must evoke, in anyone present, emotions of revulsion, anxiety, terròr, grief and the urge to render immediate help. (p. 24)

Much of the thinking Ferenczi grapples with in the *Clinical Diary* unfolded from the 1924 monograph that Ferenczi coauthored with Otto Rank, *The Development of Psychoanalysis*. In the *Clinical Diary*, Ferenczi builds on the seminal ideas presented in the monograph, challenging Freud's ideas about how the process of change takes place in psychoanalysis. Freud's earlier work from 1921 (1921/2000), "Repeating, Remembering, and Working Through," held that analysis worked by helping patients remember the early suffering they had undergone. Freud believed that unless the early suffering was lifted from repression and remembered, the patient would unwittingly repeat it. He saw any repetition in the treatment as acting out, or a form of unconscious resistance to remembering.

In *The Development of Psychoanalysis*, Ferenczi and Rank (1924), on the other hand, suggested that analysis proceeds in two phases: first the phase of reliving, or repeating, and then the phase of understanding. They argued that the more deeply repressed an early memory is, the more likely it is to find expression in reliving. Thus, they saw the reenactment of repressed memories as a form of unconscious communication, a way to let the analyst know the patient's emotional plight. As Ferenczi (1931) put it, "First you must catch the hare, then you can cook him!" (pp.131–132). By reliving early repressed experience with their analysts, patients might reconstruct their psychological lives, and, in this way, remembering can take the place of repressing, understanding the place of reliving. "This kind of therapy ... consists far more in experience than in the factor of enlightenment," Ferenczi and Rank wrote (1924, p. 56).

Ferenczi's ideas about empathy—the importance of reliving, the healing power of new experience, the commingling of suffering, the shared unconscious, and the fears analyst and patient share—all have become an integral part of my clinical work.

Matt had just put a forkful of eggs Benedict in his mouth when the first plane struck the World Trade Center and the plate glass windows came crashing into the restaurant. Today he tells me, "The other day I went down to the deli and there were some workmen just outside the front door with a jackhammer and I didn't see them and all of a sudden the jackhammer started and I just freaked. I just freak if there's a loud noise and I don't see it coming. Everything inside me shakes. I'm so scared. I'm so scared all the time I don't even know what I'm scared of anymore."

Matt doesn't look well today. There is flatness in his eyes and a kind of darkness across his face. He starts by saying, "I'm not doing too well." He goes on to describe how no place felt right anymore. When he is in his apartment reading, playing computer games, or napping, he wants to be out. When he is out he finds himself exhausted by the effort of being with people—being with them where they are doing activities that used to be his concerns but aren't anymore, at least for now, in places he used to like to be, like the noisy restaurant he went to yesterday with friends, and doing things he used to like to do, like going shopping at the Gap with his friends after lunch yesterday.

He described ending his day out with his friends at the Time Café on Broadway, happy to be in a quiet place with them. But then the glasses and silverware on the table started to rattle and the tabletop vibrated. Matt was midsentence, and he froze. He didn't know what was happening, and his mind flashed back to his breakfast meeting in the World Trade Center the morning of September 11, when the first sign that anything was wrong was that the silverware and dishes started rattling and the tables started vibrating. It lasted a few minutes. No one knew what it was. No one realized a hundred stories up a plane was about to hit the building. *Then the windows that made up the ceiling of the Greenhouse Restaurant stopped vibrating and buckled in, and Matt and the four people he was meeting with scrambled underneath their table. Matt remembers thinking, "This might be it. I might be about to die." He thought it clearly, lucidly, calmly as he looked out from under the table and saw the debris falling past the restaurant windows.*

That all came back in a flash yesterday as the number 6 train rumbled under the Time Café. Matt says, "I wanted to stand up and scream, 'I can't stay here!' But I didn't. I'd never let myself do that. But the hard part, harder than sitting there as more trains passed under the restaurant, was the fact that no one said anything. I sat there frozen, terrified, but no one said anything."

"What did they do?" I asked.

"They just started talking about something else," Matt says.

"My voice teacher says, 'Your body knows. Just get out of its way. Don't force anything, and we'll find the way for your voice to come out,'" Matt says.

"It's the same thing here," I say.

"There's just so much feeling sitting inside me and I want it to come out. It's like this black glob of feeling is inside of me and it keeps tricking me into thinking it's coming out. Then it doesn't. It doesn't want to come out. But then I see it coming out and it turns white and glowy, like something sublime. For a fleeting moment yesterday, when I was holding Alicia it felt sublime. But it's like it's afraid to come out, like maybe it's afraid if it comes out it will mean having to let go of things it shouldn't let go of."

"Like what will it have to let go of that it shouldn't?"

"Like my mother," Matt says, and his voice gets husky. "I feel panic when I say that."

"Do you know what you feel behind the panic?"

"A childish vulnerability, and then I feel self-conscious and as we're talking the new Superman song keeps going through my head."

"What words of it?"

"'I want to lie down on the sidewalk and cry. I'm not a bird, I'm not a plane....'" Matt thinks for a minute, then says, "Do you know what great psychological studies comic book characters are? Here's Superman, the most powerful person on earth but the loneliest person on earth.... He was sent by his parents to earth when their planet blew up. He looks human but he's not. He couldn't be more lonely."

"Your caring makes me feel comfortable, safe, which makes me start feeling, which makes me anxious. Alicia has been noticing how when I'm feeling a lot I check out and I'm not there. It's like the outer world fades away. There have been few moments in my life when I was feeling strongly and the outer world didn't fade away, I didn't check out," Matt says.

"Like when?" I ask.

"That time last fall when you told me you'd be here September 11. I could see you were going to say it. I knew it, then when you did everything just came flooding out of me. I felt safe, protected—that even if something happened, you would be here and I would be safe. I trust you so much, and it feels so good to just trust somebody else. But usually I don't, not when I'm feeling pain."

Matt looks down at the floor, his eyebrows furrow, and I can see his mind working. Then he says, "It's like I missed a transition in my life, so when I cry I feel like a child. It's like I never had anyone there when I was crying and not a child. Babies cry. Adults suck it up. I lived by that for a long time. It's how I got through things. But I'm an adult, and adults do cry. I don't know how to cry and feel like an adult. But I know it's possible, and I want to learn how to do it."

* * *

Ferenczi did not live long enough to arrive at the logical conclusion of his own thinking, but he was well on his way. Over and over we see him coming back to the idea of reliving. He understood that patients relived trauma from their past in the treatment, distorting their experience of the analyst in ways that conformed to their early childhoods (transference), and he understood that analysts sometimes distorted their perceptions and experience of the patient in this same way (countertransference). Because he still believed in the scientific model of analyst as objective observer, he failed to see how it was inevitable that the analyst and patient would together create, or actualize, the reality of their perceptions and experience of each other.

The patient with whom Ferenczi came closest to this understanding was Elizabeth Severn. Ferenczi (1932/1988) described his work with Severn, an American expatriate and an analyst herself:

> There was one point at which we came to loggerheads. I maintained firmly that she ought to hate me, because of my wickedness toward her [e.g., not taking the patient on vacation with him and his family, reducing the number of sessions per week from seven, indulgences he had previously allowed the patient]; she resolutely denied this, yet these denials at times were so ferocious that they always betrayed feelings of hatred. For her part she maintained that she sensed feelings of hate in me, and began saying that her analysis would never make any progress unless I allowed her to analyze those hidden feelings in me. I resisted this for approximately a year, but then I decided to make this sacrifice.
>
> To my enormous surprise I had to concede that the patient was right in many respects. I have retained from my childhood a specific anxiety with regard to strong female figures ... the patient's demands to be loved corresponded to analogous demands on me by my mother. In actual fact, and inwardly, therefore, I did hate the patient in spite of all the friendliness I displayed; this was what she was aware of, to which she reacted with the same inaccessibility that had finally forced her criminal father to renounce her. (pp. 98–99)

So Ferenczi dedicated himself to the experiment he called *mutual analysis* with Elizabeth Severn. The analysis was mutual in that both were analyzing as well as being analyzed, but I think what they did would be better termed *parallel analysis*. A mutual analysis would have included not only analyzing each of their individual lives but also, just as important, analyzing what each of them had contributed to their shared experience. For instance, in addition to looking at Ferenczi's propensity to hate strong women and Severn's to bear hateful feelings toward men due to her father, they would have looked at how each of them out of their own lives contributed to the dynamic of hatred between them, a dynamic that both of them needed to relive in order to raise it from repression and to repair it.

What function and purpose did this serve each of them in his or her own way? Could Severn only come to know her own hatred of her father and his hatred of her by stimulating it in Ferenczi? Did she unconsciously want to be renounced by Ferenczi as she had by "her criminal father"? In the *Clinical Diary* Ferenczi (1932/1988) stated, "[M]y refusal of love toward my mother became displaced onto the patients" (p. 86). Does the pain behind this statement also lie behind Ferenczi's hatred of Severn? Did Ferenczi recoil from her not only as a matter of his own history of having an overbearing mother but also because unconsciously he was responding to Severn's re-creation in him of her father's feelings—feelings she had to re-create in order to come to know them really fully for the first time in consciousness? Perhaps bringing her relationship with Ferenczi to the brink of collapse was what Severn needed to do, this time in order to learn how to emotionally repair, restore, and reconstitute a damaged relationship.

After Matt leaves, I sit in the window seat of my office looking out over Grace Episcopal Church. I watch the willow tree in the church-yard sway in the breeze and think about what to do. Matt says he's staying here September 11. He says the day is not about fear for him. For Matt, it's about grieving his loss and the world's loss, and it's about healing. How can I not be here for him?

"I'm getting more emotional about September 11. I realized today I've lost my appetite and I haven't been eating the last 2 days. I don't know who's going to be there for me Wednesday. I don't think Dad. He's offered to take me out for lunch, but I don't think he's really going to be able to be there for me. And I don't even think my sister will be able to. Alicia will be as much as she can, but she has so much going on herself. She has her first therapy appointment, and she's really nervous about that," Matt says.

"When you think of someone being there for you, how do you see them being there for you?" I ask.

"Someone who just knows what you need, you don't need to ask, like a mother would know, but I don't think anyone is going to be that for me. I'm going to have to be that for myself on Wednesday."

I want to tell him I'm going to be there for him Wednesday. I hesitate, wonder if I should, if it's self-aggrandizing or seductive or something, but I only hesitate for a moment. Most of me feels, "Tell him." He needs to know someone's there for him, that he doesn't have to do this for himself, and so I say, "I don't know if I should tell you this, but I had no intention of being in the city on Wednesday. I don't want to be here and I assumed you wouldn't be here either—that you would be out in New Jersey—and so when you told me you were going to be here, it threw me a curveball and I'm going to come back Wednesday night to see you because I want to be here with you."

Matt closes his eyes and weeps. When he speaks again he says, "This isn't confusing, but you look so much like my mother sometimes it's difficult."

I nod.

"You don't act like her, but you look like her."

"I don't act like her? I thought I did."

"Well, I didn't know you knew that."

"You've let me know that."

"Well, I didn't want to say it because I didn't know if you would want to be in that role, if that would be okay with you."

I smile.

"That's okay with you?"

"Yeah, that's okay with me," I say, but as I say it I hear the tightness in my voice. Mostly it is okay with me, and I want it to be completely okay with me, but there is still a part of me that pulls back.

After Matt leaves I sit in the window seat and put my head back against the wall, close my eyes, and try to feel my way back into the tightness I heard in my voice. I feel my throat and chest constrict, and then I feel the moment just before that. There was still a part of me that pulled back from need, and in that moment of connecting to Matt's need and feeling the soothing, comforting response inside me, I think I connected to my own need and pulled away.

I think of Matt telling me how he'd found his mother's journal after her death. One day she had written that she was uncertain whether her children loved her or not. Matt was stunned that that lay behind his mother's reserve.

Kathy, a good friend from graduate school, and I sit in the park by the Hudson River for a while and then have an early dinner. That night at dinner we talk about the past year, the fact that it's September 11 today, how good it feels that this day is almost over, what it's been like, what it's like today. I thank her for being there, for all those mornings of picking up her phone in her office and talking me through, listening to me through, my fear, my pain, my upset. The mornings I woke up terrified, the mornings I woke up feeling like a robot. The morning I woke up weeping—dialing her office in Rockland County and her picking up the phone.

I tell her that for me, she embodies an editorial on courage that was in the New York Times *a few days after last September 11. It said all different kinds of courage were going to be required in the coming days. One form that would be needed was for people to have the courage to look at a person who'd lost someone at the World Trade Center in the eye and feel the pain that comes from making that connection. That's the kind of courage she has had with me.*

She says, "It was easy to do because of the way you approached me and allowed me to give to you in ways I never could before. Do you remember the time in graduate school in the Rathskeller when I was upset about Rich rejecting me?"

I wince and nod yes, recalling how I feel that I failed her then. She'd gone back to him after he'd rejected her, and I told her what she needed to do was to stop wanting anything from him and not let him know it hurt to cut herself off from him.

She continues, "You're so different from that now. I've never seen you allow yourself to be as vulnerable as you have this past year. You were so open to the hurt that was all around you. You took it in from other people, and you didn't spit it back out. You let it seep into yourself, and then you asked for help with it from other people. I felt honored that you turned to me. You allowed me to give to you in ways you never could before. You let yourself be so vulnerable and needful."

* * *

Ferenczi's idea of reliving anticipated the contemporary psychoanalytic idea of enactment. In the diary Ferenczi (1932/1988) said, "The time will come when he [the analyst] will have to repeat with his own hands the act of murder previously perpetrated against the patient" (p. 52). Sooner or later, the analyst will actually injure the patient as he or she has been injured before. This is not a matter of a distorted perception of the analyst brought about by transference. In these moments the analyst in actuality wounds the patient in the very way he or she has feared. What makes the difference is how the two of them deal with it afterwards. Reparation is crucial. In fact, in his last entry in *The Clinical Diary* Ferenczi said, "I released RN [Elizabeth Severn] from her torments by repeating the sins of her father, which I then confessed and for which I obtained forgiveness" (p. 214).

Is this the heart of psychoanalysis? Are we not always looking for these moments of repetition and reparation? Searching for a new way out of the past into the present?

Matt picked up his headshots earlier in the day and is feeling good about them, about how he looks and how relaxed he was during the photo shoot. The photographer said she thought they'd come out great, and she wished all her clients were like Matt. "She might say that to everyone—but I don't think so," Matt says, grinning.

Partway into the session Matt says, "Boy, it's hot in here." The heat blasts into my office in the winter, and I have no way to regulate it except to keep the window open. He gets up and pulls off his black wool turtleneck. Underneath he wears a gray short-sleeve silk T-shirt. A tuft of hair sprouts over the top of the T-shirt. He prides himself on his body. Although he isn't tall, he is muscular and firm. He works out with weights and it shows, especially now sitting here in his short-sleeve silk T-shirt in the middle of January. He is showing off his body to me. He knows it, and I know it. And I think he knows I know it. I am acutely aware of his body, how muscular his arms and chest are.

Matt arrives a half hour late for his appointment, explaining he was at a voice lesson and both he and the teacher lost track of the time because they were so "into it." Last week he was 15 minutes late one day, explaining he'd gone out running and gotten back late. That same day he confirmed the time of our appointment the next day, a new appointment time, but then mixed up the time and arrived 2 hours late for it.

I sit in the window seat looking out at the rain falling and the sea of mostly black umbrellas below and wonder about what's going on with

Matt. *I wonder about what he might be trying to avoid. Perhaps if he's trying to communicate something, and the frustration and annoyance I feel are ways he has of telling me something about his frustration and annoyance. Then, too, I thought maybe he has sensed a change in me and it is scaring him.*

I used my recent turn to present in my consultation group to review my work with Matt. Over the last 3 weeks of talking with Alan, Debbie, Melinda, and Phil about my work with Matt I have come to have a much deeper realization of how connected I feel to Matt and how much I care about him.

In fact, the connection between Matt and me was a focus of the consultation. The first week I presented, Phil said he was struck by how present I am to Matt, how much I am right there in the moment feeling with him and for him. I was surprised when Phil said that. Part of me said, "Huh?" but another part of me said, "Yeah. I'm there. I'm very there." It was much like one day when Matt said to me, "That's what I love about you. You care so much and are so passionate about what you do." I was taken aback and thought, "I do?" Yes, I do, but there's some way I'm disconnected from my caring and our connection. Phil said he thought he understood—that it is like I need to create a reflective space for my caring, a space where I reflect on my own internal experience and connect to it, so I feel myself as the agent of the experience, that I am the self doing the caring and in that space I own the caring. It's a funny thought—convoluted to think that I don't feel connected to what I'm actually feeling, and feeling intensely, but it was true of me in this regard and was beginning to change.

And I wonder if Matt is feeling the change in me, feeling me to be more connected and more involved with him increasingly over the past few weeks, and if that's scaring him. As a matter of fact, Phil pointed out in our group that in a recent session Matt was feeling vulnerable and I responded to his anxiety and he moved away. I wonder if it's feeling a little too much for him right now, if he can't put his finger on it so we can talk about it, but if he's feeling me as even more present and as much as he wants that there's another part of him that it makes anxious and he moves away.

* * *

Ferenczi put great stock in the idea of the therapeutic relationship as a healing experience. Along with Freud he saw interpretation on the analyst's part, and coming to insight on the patient's part, as curative. But he went beyond this, to the idea of the relationship in and of itself as healing. He believed that psychological pain and symptomatology had their roots in experiences in relationships and could be healed by new experience in different relationships:

> Should it even occur, and it does occasionally to me, that experiencing another's and my own suffering brings a tear to my eye (and one should not conceal this emotion from the patient). Then the tears of doctor and of patient mingle in a sublimated communion which perhaps finds its analogy only in the mother-child relationship. And this is the healing agent, which, like a kind of glue, binds together permanently the intellectually assembled fragments, surrounding even the personality thus repaired with a new aura of vitality and optimism. (1932/1988, p. 65)

Matt and I talk about how much he's been playing the video game Everquest—*up to 8, 10 hours a day—and how he feels like he can't stop. He tells me how hard it is to be with himself, to spend time alone without feeling lonely, and how he goes on the Internet and starts to play* Everquest. *Sometimes he reads to get away from his loneliness. I ask him if he ever reads as a way of being with himself, of getting to know himself better rather than as a way to escape himself. He says there is one book he's read recently that is like that, a book that takes him into rather than away from himself. It is called* The Notebook *(Sparks, 1996). It is about a woman who has Alzheimer's. After she's diagnosed, before her memory deteriorates badly, she and her husband sit down and write the story of their relationship together. Then, as she progressively loses her memory her husband reads the story to her. "By the end of the book they're both in the same nursing home together and the wife hardly remembers who her husband is, but every afternoon he reads the story of their relationship to her," Matt says.*

An image of my father sitting in his wheelchair in the nursing home, barely able to speak anymore, comes into my mind, and my eyes fill with tears.

Matt asks, "What's wrong?"

I tell him, "My dad has Alzheimer's."

He says, "My grandmother had it, too. I'm sorry."

He pauses, and then starts talking about his mother's dying, telling me things he's never told me before. The day she died, he went back to school. The entire family was at the hospital. They knew her death was imminent.

"I wish I'd stayed at the hospital," Matt says. "I feel so bad I didn't stay. Mom would have stayed for me. My aunt told me I should stay."

"What did you say?"

"Something like 'Go to hell.' I have so many regrets around Mom's death," Matt says.

He tells me about scattering his mom's ashes over the lake in front of their family's summer home in Maine. Matt and his dad and younger sister took her ashes out in a canoe. The container for the ashes was a cheap plasticene box the crematorium had put them in. Matt took the stern and paddled and steered the canoe, while his dad and sister took handfuls of ashes and scattered them over the lake. "I didn't want to touch them," Matt says.

"I wish that I had touched them," Matt says just before we have to stop. And when he gets to the door, he throws his backpack over his shoulder and says, "I wish that I had touched them."

Matt tells me about its being his 25th birthday today and how he has always tried to act like his birthday was no big deal, but, then again, how today is a special day for him. He is going to dinner with his dad and stepmother tonight. Matt's eyes drift off, and his speech slows down. I ask him what is happening. "I'm just thinking about Mom," he says. "I wish she were alive. I wish she was going to be there tonight at dinner."

Then he stops talking and looks down at his backpack, saying, "This feels kind of awkward, but ..." and reaches in, pulls out a book, and hands it to me.

He says, "I bought this for you." It is a copy of The Notebook *(Sparks, 1996). I don't feel discomfort or a need to explore what giving the gift to me is about. It feels right. It feels okay.*

I sit quietly and simply say, "Thank you."

Matt says he'd thought about it from the moment he left, and I ask what it is he'd thought.

He chokes up and then says, "You remind me so much of my mother. It's so hard and so confusing. You even look like her. She was tall and strong. She rode horses and was so full of life. She was smart and had a doctorate. I miss her so much. She's missed so much in my life, and I haven't had a mother I could talk to. I haven't had a mother I could tell about my dreams of acting, or how well I've done at work, or how insecure I feel about my looks, or how anxious I feel just asking a girl out. And now," he hesitates, "I feel like I kind of do."

Wrapped in the white afghan from my couch, I sit in the window seat on my break leafing through The Notebook *(Sparks, 1996) and thinking about Matt. I think of how he is the age of some of my friends' and siblings' children and of how he has the handsome dark Irish looks of my father and one of my brothers, and wonder if I'd had a son if he might have looked like Matt.*

* * *

Ferenczi felt tremendous empathy for his patients, and they seem to have been more likely to enter states of regression than Freud's. Ferenczi also believed that patients who were quite deprived in childhood may need an initial, sometimes lengthy, period in treatment where their childhood wishes are indulged and gratified in ways they'd never before been.

One day in a session with an adult male patient, the patient suddenly got up from the couch and threw his arms around Ferenczi's neck, saying, "Oh Grandpa, I am afraid I will have a baby" (Ferenczi, 1931, pp. 129–130). Ferenczi joined the regression and played out the patient's fantasy that he would have a baby. When Ferenczi later referred to this moment as "a game," his patient objected to the trivialization implied. Ferenczi wrote that his patient was correct and there were serious realities they had worked with through the fantasy.

When I open the door, Matt is sitting with his headphones on, his head bobbing up and down to the music. He gives me a slight smile as he walks in, tosses his red backpack on the floor next to him, and slouches into the chair. Matt doesn't ever sit down in the chair—he slouches, slumps, plops, or throws himself into it. He never just sits down into it. And he always carries his red backpack—ever since last September. "I don't need this," he said one day to me as he set his backpack down. "It's not like I need it to carry anything in. Most of the time I come here from home and go back home or to acting class, but ever since September 11 I carry it with me when I go out. It's like taking a little bit of home with me when I go."

"*What do you carry in it?*" *I asked, wondering what objects comprised a bit of home for him. I was aware Matt always had his backpack with him, but I hadn't put together that it had only been since last September.*

"*All kinds of stuff. A bunch of pens, a few pencils, my cell phone, something to write in,*" *he said, pulling out a small brown leather journal,* "*my CD player, a book,*" *he said, pulling out a book of poetry by Charles Bukowski, whom he'd come to know and like over the past year,* "*always a book. If I'm reading, like on the subway, I forget about where I am and I don't feel afraid.*"

As Matt settles back into the chair today he says, "*I can't think about the World Trade Center without crying.*"

"*What are you feeling?*"

Matt stops and reflects. "*Not afraid. It doesn't feel like fear. Sad. I feel sad at the weight of the whole tragedy and for my own personal loss. I feel like I'm crying for the kid who ran away from the World Trade Center and spent the next week alone in New Jersey and just sort of hid away. And I want to be here next week for the ceremony at Ground Zero. I want to stand there while they read the names of all twenty-eight hundred people who died there. I've thought of asking Dad to go with me, but I think it would make it harder, harder for me to feel. I feel so sad about it. I feel like I want to go to the ceremony that morning and have some anonymous person, some stranger, look at me and think, 'Look at that kid who's falling apart,' and then put their arms around me.*"

* * *

Ferenczi's empathy was exquisite, rooted as it was in his own openness to self:

Certain phases of mutual analysis give the impression of two equally terrified children who compare their experiences, and because of their common fate, understand each other completely and instinctively try to comfort each other. Awareness of the shared fate allows the partner to appear as completely harmless, therefore as someone whom one can trust with confidence. (1932/1988, p. 56)

"It's so hard going on this way every day and with so few people knowing or understanding—really only you and Alicia and my sister. Dad tries but he doesn't really get it. On the subway today on the way home from class, I looked around at each person on the car asking myself if they came at me if I could take them. There was only one guy I didn't think I could—a guy built like me and he scared me. And then I came home and told Alicia I just needed her to hold me. I had that feeling again that behind all that fear I just want to cry."

"It's probably a feeling you've had all your life behind your anxiety."

"Yeah. I think it's because I know I've been scared much of my life and you can't cry when you're in the jungle."

"And sometimes when you get out of the jungle, you don't even know it."

"Right. You have all these defenses built up, telling yourself you're not scared, showing other people you're not scared, and you're scared all the time."

Today Matt says, "If someone had said to me before I came here that they could cure my panic attacks in 16 sessions or cure my fear of going outside my apartment in 16 sessions I would have gone to them. I know that the cognitive-behaviorist psychologists claim they cure people that quickly, and there's no symptom substitution that occurs. I wonder. Do they? The way the research is designed, it's slanted toward symptoms only. I wonder if people are actually better. I know psychoanalysis works. I'm living proof of it. But it's hard work; it's really hard work. It takes a long time and there's so much pain involved in it. But I didn't only get over my panic attacks or agoraphobia. I've discovered who I am—and I'm still discovering it. And during this whole time you never told me who I was. You helped me discover it. It's like you brought me to the edge but I had to come to things myself. I was talking to my dad about my expenses for next year, and I said, 'Analysis is really expensive.' He said, 'It's the best thing you've ever done. I've got my old Matt back.' I really have mixed feelings when he says that. One of the things I've learned is there are many Matts, not just one."

* * *

One of the most interesting ideas for me in Ferenczi's diary (1932/1988) is that of a shared unconscious. Ferenczi actually attributed this idea to his patient Elizabeth Severn. Upon telling Ferenczi a dream, she said she thought of it as an expression of her and Ferenczi's shared unconscious, one that is "a combination of the unconscious contents of the psyches of the analysand and the analyst." We analysts are used to thinking of our patients as having an unconscious and ourselves as having one as well, and to the ongoing "dialogue of unconsciouses" that underlies our conscious communications with each other. But what about the notion that our patients and we create a shared unconscious that emerges out of our relationship with each other? Jungians believe in a collective unconscious that transcends all individuals. Why not a dyadic unconscious growing out of one's relationship with another?

Matt tells me he's had a nightmare about September 11 for the first time since that day. He says he dreamed he was in an airplane. He thinks he was trying to fix something in the airplane and it crashed. It landed just off an island. A huge tidal wave started coming toward him. He got up onto a bluff on the island before the tidal wave hit, and he could see there were more coming, one right after the other. Off in the distance on an isthmus was a big city. It had been hit by a nuclear bomb and was falling apart, disintegrating. All the buildings were falling down. The tidal wave washed over the bluff and over Matt. He was able to keep his head above water but woke up terrified. He lay in bed reminding himself one by one of each person sleeping in the house that night—his aunt, his uncle, and his cousins.

I had my first dream that I remember about the World Trade Center. In it I was on my way to work in Chicago, going down the Lincoln Park Lagoon on a boat to the Loop. I looked up and saw smoke billowing from the Sears Towers. It had been blown up. Chicago was under attack. Pandemonium broke out. I was a couple of miles from home. I could walk west and try to get a cab or head east and try to get on a commuter boat headed north on Lake Michigan. I walked west to Clark Street, but all the cabs were already taken. By the time I got over to the lake, the lines for the boats were long. All I wanted was to get home. I felt afraid and far away, but I reminded myself that I was only a couple of miles from home and could walk home to safety.

After seeing Matt in session today, the end of the dream comes back to mind, the part about how it's only a couple of miles to home. I think of Matt and think, "Maybe the mother you see in me and long for will be there when I get home."

5 Harold and Uncle Frank

Several months into treatment, Harold started a session by telling me how the previous evening he and his wife had gone to a performance by the Chicago Symphony Orchestra at Orchestra Hall. When they got back to their building, the regular doorman wasn't there. He'd gotten ill, and someone who had never worked the building before was filling in for him. The doorman stopped Harold and said he needed to see some identification. Harold explained he was a tenant in the building, and the doorman said he was sorry, but because he didn't know Harold or his wife he would need to see some ID. When Harold started for the elevator, the doorman stepped in front of him.

"What did you do?" I asked.

"I took him by the collar, shoved him up against the wall, and told him, 'I'm Harold P. Stendahl. I live in apartment 10E, and if you know what's good for you, you'll stand right here while my wife and I go get on the elevator.'" Once in the elevator, Harold's wife told him she couldn't believe how the doorman was only doing his job and Harold had completely humiliated him. Harold told his wife that, when they walked into the building, the doorman "didn't see tenants walking in. He saw niggers walking in." He said there was no way the doorman would have asked for ID from a White man wearing a suit, carrying a briefcase, and walking in with his wife.

Harold's wife said it wasn't the fact that Harold had gotten angry that upset her; it was the way he'd gotten angry that was so upsetting. Harold didn't understand. He didn't know how he might have gotten angry differently. He said his wife "just didn't get it." When they got up to their apartment, she packed a suitcase and said that she was going to stay with her sister for a while, because she was too terrified to be around him anymore.

Harold and I had had some rows and made it through them, so that I thought he would be able to hear where I was coming from if I took up what it must have been like for his wife. I asked Harold how strong his anger had been compared to what I'd seen in sessions with him. He said it was about half of what I'd experienced, explaining his wife was "very fragile." I said, "A lot of people couldn't tolerate half of what I've seen here, Harold."

Harold's anger reminded me of the kind of anger I'd grown up with in my father, sudden and intense. I knew that anger. Sometimes it filled me, too. It felt scary. It felt intimidating, and I'd be damned if I'd ever be intimidated again in that way, so when Harold walked into the office in that aura of rage, I went right up against him, matching his intense, focused energy with my own, letting him know I wouldn't be cowed by him. I worried that it would be better for Harold to be with someone who could leave more of an open space for Harold's rage, or feel his or her own fear more in the face of it, and I also knew I could not and would not do that. Maybe one day I would be able to, but not now.

When Harold first came to see me, we had an extended consultation period lasting a couple of months before I committed to working with him on a long-term basis. A subtle wave of sadness washed over his face the day I told him I was uncertain as to whether or not I could work with him and would need more time to decide.

"This is a familiar place," he said, "but at least here it's on the table."

"I don't know that there's another place we can be right now," I said.

Harold nodded, then said, "Well, at least I know now what the journey is I have to take."

* * *

Harold was going to need to relive his rage in the treatment with me if any healing was to take place. He would need to reexperience it with me in order to rework it. That meant he would come to feel devalued by me both as a person, as he had with his father, and as an African American man, as he had in society, in order to reach a different place with his rage and others' destructiveness.

On my part, I would need to "become the murderer this time" (Ferenczi, 1933/1988, p. 52), as Sándor Ferenczi put it. There would be moments in our relationship in which, unwittingly, I would become the instrument of degradation and the object of Harold's rage.

Every time Harold talked about either his father beating him or the mistreatment and discrimination he'd suffered as a Black man, I felt like I wanted to weep. I could not imagine what it must be like to see women cross the street to avoid you, hear car locks go down as you approach cars at the intersection, watch taxicabs fly by you refusing to pick you up, and be followed around expensive stores by security guards or stopped by one in your own building. I filled with an enormous grief and sadness and felt like I knew him deeply. In those moments I felt connected to the person behind the rage. Along with that, I felt that anyone was going to meet Harold's rage with their own personal limitations and defenses and that would be part of both people's working things through in the dyad, and so I agreed to work with Harold and we began twice-weekly appointments.

* * *

A recurring theme in our work was Harold's feeling that he didn't know who he was or what he wanted in life. He started one session by saying, "I don't know what I want." I'd thought he was referring to therapy, but he was referring to life—everything from his job to what he wanted to do on a Saturday morning, he told me.

"And I have an active social life," he said. "I get invitations to things and I just keep RSVPing, but I don't know what I really want. If you told me you'd give me a 2-week vacation all expenses paid to anywhere I wanted to go right now, I would have no idea where that would be."

No one had ever helped him really know who he was. There were clear expectations he achieve, use his intelligence, go to good schools, and be polite and courteous. Within that, he carved out a sense of his own identity by being rebellious and rule breaking at the same time as he achieved high grades, got an excellent job, and had flawless manners.

But he didn't know who he really was. I asked if anyone had ever helped him really know what his gifts were, his characteristics, his qualities, who he was as a unique person, and help him develop as that person. He said, "No." I hoped that was part of where we'd go in the treatment.

* * *

I dealt with Harold's insistence on standing until I was seated in different ways on different days. Sometimes I went ahead and sat down first. Sometimes I waited him out, usually having to prod him by saying, "Go ahead. Have a seat." We'd talked about it. He explained he was a "very formal and deferential" person. I suggested his manners, his highly elaborated code of conduct, helped to keep his anger in check. He agreed.

One day I dallied by the door a few seconds and he stood by his chair. I kidded him. In a joking way I said, "Come on. You can do it. You can sit down first."

He looked at me and smiled. "Should I?" he said.

"Yeah. Should I give you a drum roll?" I asked.

"That would be great,"" he said. We sat down laughing.

And then he told me the story of the putter. He'd gone on a golf vacation to Miami with a friend since I'd last seen him.

"I broke my putter in half," he said.

"That's pretty hard to do," I said.

"Not really, not if I take it and hit the putting green with it with all my might."

Harold had played football in college. He had massive shoulders and thick thighs. When he got up to leave at the end of sessions he often limped a little, like athletes who've worn out the cartilage in their knees do.

I imagined the green. They were playing a really nice course, he said. The green must have been smooth like a velvet carpet and as delicate as well. If he hit the green with so much force it broke his putter, he must have really done some damage to the green itself. He wouldn't be seated before a woman was, but he'd throw his putter at the putting green. Golf etiquette dictated you didn't even set the head of another club on a putting green. You either left it on the apron of the green where the grass was a little thicker, or you laid the head of the club on the pin the flag flew on, and rested only the grip of the club on the green so that you wouldn't mar the surface of the green. People carry picks with them to fix the green after they've finished the hole. They look like two-pronged hair picks. You dig them into the ground around the mark your ball made on the green when you chipped up onto it and you gently press on it, bringing the indentation from the ball mark back up level with the rest of the green so later players aren't set off course by the slight depression in the green that your ball has made. For good golfers, this is a big deal.

I was struck by the ironies involved in each of our reactions. Harold felt all right about shoving someone up against the wall and hammering a green with his putter, but wouldn't sit down before a woman sat first. I could completely understand Harold shoving the doorman, was mildly annoyed by his insistence I be seated before him, but was shocked by his deliberately pounding the green.

* * *

One day I could see Harold standing outside my office door, ringing the buzzer. He glared at me as I walked down the hall toward him.

"I'm sorry to keep you," I said.

Harold didn't respond. Walking into my office he threw his briefcase down on the floor, waited for me to sit, then sat down himself. He looked at the clock and said, "We're starting late."

The force of anger in his voice and eyes took me aback when he spoke.

"I was in the bathroom," I said.

"And I stood outside in the hall, ringing the buzzer and waiting to be buzzed in, and it isn't the first time it's happened."

"Harold, if you'd been here before I went out to the bathroom I would have let you in. Otherwise, it would be a couple of minutes."

"That's not acceptable," Harold said, slamming his fist on the arm of the chair.

I sat quietly for a few moments, looking at Harold, realizing just how enraged he was. Part of me felt scared by his fury, and that only made me angry and determined to fight this out with him, whatever this was.

"Harold, what's really going on with you today?"

"There's nothing going on with me today. Everything was fine until I got here."

"All your rage can't be about my not being here to buzz you in and starting a minute late."

"It really pissed me off. It was like being reduced to a young schoolboy."

"Do you think your reaction has anything to do with how reduced and belittled you were by your father growing up?"

"I don't think it has a thing to do with it," Harold said and walked out of the office. "Save your fancy interpretations for someone else."

Two days later, Harold returned for what was our usual second weekly appointment. I was in the office when he rang and buzzed him in. He came into my office looking a little sheepish and said, "I suppose we should talk about what happened here the other day."

"We should," I said.

"It was like what I told you happens to me in restaurants. If I ask the waiter for something and it doesn't come and I have to ask a second time, I want to tear the guy from limb to limb."

"How is that like the other day?"

"The waiting. Being ignored, dismissed, set aside."

"Did you feel all those things the other day waiting outside the door?"

"Yes. I did."

"I can see how you'd feel annoyed, irritated, even slighted, but the intensity of your anger was so strong," I said.

"That sounds like what my wife says to me—that it isn't just getting angry that's the problem. It's that I get so angry."

It was a complicated psychological and social enactment at the door. Harold and I failed to acknowledge it as a racial enactment, much less reflect upon it in an effort to understand how it was working within and between us. I was aware of my own idiosyncratic way of reacting to another's anger with fear, followed quickly by anger and determination not to allow myself to be dominated. Undoubtedly, the combination of Harold being big, Black, and male all intensified my reaction. I suggested Harold look to his own similar individual transferential pattern of feeling belittled and then furious. My interpretation of Harold's rage at the door was only in terms of his familial upbringing, I had blinders on to society's mistreatment of him enacted again with me in that moment. The opportunity to come to a deeper understanding of the preconscious or unconscious racial (or gender or power) attitudes and reactions enacted between us was lost. In the end, I named the intensity of Harold's anger as the culprit and he accepted it, foreclosing further exploration on either of our parts. Had I been more aware of the complexities of the emotional situation between Harold and me at that moment, we might have realized we were in a racial as well as personal enactment that, if recognized, had the potential for new ways of being for both Harold and me. Throughout his treatment, we never spoke about the fact that Harold was Black and I was White.

Powerlessness and control, privilege and rejection, aggressive and libidinal impulses—the subject of race raises all of these reactions. It is no wonder that, traditionally, matters of race went largely unaddressed in psychoanalysis. Race was regarded as a sociological rather than psychological phenomenon, hence, outside the purview of psychoanalysis. Under this silence rumbled anxieties about such raw human feeling. Then, too, one feared being perceived as or "caught at" being or saying something racist, just as the other feared being devalued or marginalized yet again in life. Psychoanalytic articles about race were rare. Race was ideally thought to be transcended by those involved in interracial relationships. Color was only skin deep.

But, of course, it isn't, and psychoanalysis has caught up with that reality. Racial enactments—"interactive sequences embodying the actualization in the clinical situation of cultural attitudes towards race and race difference"—are inevitable, and silence is probably the most common of racial enactments (Leary, 2000). The aim in treatment is to own racial enactments in order to examine them together. We struggle to accept that we have racist thoughts and feelings, realizing that at this time in our culture each of us carries within ourselves some of the tensions, stereotypes, and prejudices of our own society. "It seems inevitable that each of us will, at one time or another drift into unintended racial thoughts, feelings and actions" (Leary, 2000). Moreover,

> [I]t seems inevitable that all of us—patients and analysts—will have racial thoughts and feelings that are libidinally and aggressively tinged.... It is also quite likely that the patient will, in time, catch the analyst in some unintended racial reflection of his or her own. (Leary, 1997)

In a series of papers written in the past several years (1995, 1997a, 1997b, 2000a, 2000b), psychoanalyst Kimberlyn Leary urged us toward collaborative methods of approaching race in treatment. The goal is not the elimination of enacted prejudice from the consulting room. Rather, the aim would be to give it full credence … to accept the racial enactment and submit to it sustained reflection in order to examine and understand how it operates and works. (2000)

To live with racial enactments means to accept that:

> They encompass considerably more than "mistakes of the head", e.g., inattention to knowledge about other cultures. They also emanate from the sore spots in the heart that are the legacy of social history of race in the United States (cf. Morrison, 1992). It is a history to which each of us is heir. (2000, p. 652)

* * *

Uncle Frank started an organization named the "Ragen Colts." It was an athletic organization, a neighborhood athletic club, one of many in Chicago in the early 1900s. It was composed of White teenagers and young men in their 20s from Canaryville. The other large athletic association on the South side at the time was the "Hamburgs" from Bridgeport, just north of Canaryville, and their president was Richard J. Daley.

Uncle Frank wasn't my uncle actually. He was my great-uncle and a man I never met. I met Uncle Mike and Aunt Minnie, his brother and sister, but I never met Uncle Frank. Dad stiffened at the rare mention of Uncle Frank. In the one family photograph I saw of Uncle Frank, he was wearing a loud, floral print tie.

I knew some people thought the Ragen Colts weren't just an athletic organization, and when I taught sociology at McAuley High School I did a unit on juvenile delinquency. The *Chicago Tribune* had special educational newspapers on specific topics and sent them to teachers to use with their students. One of the issues I ordered from them was the issue on juvenile delinquency, and I arrived at school one morning to find a couple of stacks of them at my classroom door. On the back page of the paper was an article entitled "The First Juvenile Delinquent Gang in Chicago History: The Ragen Colts." I thought it was pretty fascinating, kind of cool even. I was 23 years old, and it seemed like a movie to me. It was only when I got older that I started identifying more with the previous generations of my family, with these people I never knew, and felt like they somehow reflected on me. I remember telling the first group of kids I taught that morning that that was my great-uncle Frank who'd started that gang, that presumably first gang of juvenile delinquents in Chicago. They thought I was joking.

It wasn't until years later, late one night at a family party, my brother Tim told me Uncle Frank and the Ragen Colts had been involved in the race riots in Chicago in 1919. I assumed what Tim had heard was a rumor that over the years had taken on the status of fact in the lore of the old South side. It was some time after that I walked by the window of the Northwestern University bookstore and saw the book *Race Riot: Chicago in the Red Summer of 1919* by William M. Tuttle, Jr. (1996). I was on my way to lunch. I paused and thought about going in, then thought the better of it and went down the block to the Unicorn Café. Each day for the next several days when I went to lunch, I glanced at the bookstore window as I walked by, thought about going in to look at the book to see if there was anything about Uncle Frank in it, but I kept going. Then one day I decided to go in.

The book was in the back of the store. There were dozens of them. It was required reading for a course that fall on race relations. The summer of 1919 was known as the Red Summer, with race riots erupting around the world. During and after the First World War, there was a massive influx of Southern Black immigrants to the industrial cities, including Chicago. Although jobs were plentiful, housing was not, and, as the numbers of Black immigrants grew, they began purchasing homes in what were formerly all-White neighborhoods and using public properties and recreational spaces that had historically been used exclusively by White people. Racial tensions were enormous, and a turf fight between Blacks and Whites at the 29th Street Beach in which a Black boy drowned exploded into 4 days of rioting throughout the city, leaving 23 Blacks and 15 Whites dead with hundreds more injured. The author said he wrote the book from "the bottom up," trying to convey the lived experience of the people of Chicago, rather than from the "top down," more of an analysis of failed governmental policies.

I opened to the index in the back. Uncle Frank's name was there, a few pages referenced to him. The first page I opened to talked about how Uncle Frank testified before a commission on discrimination. He testified about the discrimination against Catholics by the Ku Klux Klan on the South side of Chicago. "There," I thought. "He not only hadn't done anything wrong, he was one of the people discriminated against."

I turned to the next page that was cited in the index. It described the evening of July 30, 1919, on the South side of Chicago:

> Above all was the fear of a widespread plot to burn the black belt; the fire department reported 37 conflagrations in five hours that evening, many of them set within a few minutes on the same block. At 51st Street and Shields Avenue, for example, three blocks west of Wentworth, there had been for years a black enclave of nine families, but that night the Ragen Colts tried to burn it to the ground. Throughout the afternoon, reported Harriett White, one of the block residents, there had been rumors of a mob that intended "to run all of the niggers out of this section tonight." Repeated phone calls to the police had brought only a brief visit by about ten mounted policemen at 6:30. Two hours later the Colts arrived, 200 strong and they started throwing rocks, bricks, and other missiles and shooting into ... houses.... Then they began storming through the front doors, smashing furniture and throwing it through windows, and putting the torch to everything. "Bricks, stones, and shots entered my home, forcing me to leave," recalled Mrs. White. Having done their work, the Colts left a warning: "if you open your mouth against Ragen's we will not only burn your house down, we will 'do' you." (Tuttle, 1996, pp. 54–55)

My head spun, and I held on to the bookcase to steady myself.

How could I write this, disclose this venom? How would Harold react if he knew? If I were Harold, I'd get up and leave and never come back. I sat across from Harold in sessions haunted by the knowledge of Uncle Frank's actions. Harold told me about the insults hurled against him in the course of his daily living, and I wondered how he would react to knowing this was in my family history. Would he forgive? Where does forgiveness begin? Would he try to see it with the eyes of 1919? Would that make any difference? Does it make any difference? But it wasn't my father or my grandfather who did this. It was my grandfather's younger brother, whom my father hated.

What was it in me that led me to carry the shame of Uncle Frank? What did I need to come to terms with in myself? At my sister Mary's wedding some years ago, a man going through the receiving line shook my father's hand and asked if he was related to the Ragen Colts. My father wordlessly shook the man's hand, then turned to the next guest in line.

"I've always told your father he has nothing to be ashamed of. It was other people who committed those horrible acts, not he," my mother once told me.

"I know how Dad feels, though. I feel that way, too," I said.

What became of Mrs. White? Did she have children? If so, where are her great-grandchildren now, two generations later? What can I do now that would make a difference? Is there something I could do? Is there any room for reparation in something like this? I want to tell Harold I am so sorry. Given the historical and present treatment of African Americans in the United States, no wonder Harold is angry and brittle and defensive. How could one not be finally enraged?

I recall a conversation with a man I dated who was very active in South Africa in the anti-apartheid movement in the 1980s. "How can you be so involved without being consumed by rage?" I asked. He answered, "The point isn't to get angry. The point is to prevail."

That same evening, he took my hand as we carried lawn chairs and a picnic basket to an outdoor concert in Grant Park. A White man sitting on a blanket with a woman and two children glared with an intensity that was unnerving. At first I felt confused and perplexed. It didn't dawn on me until later that his hatred was triggered by seeing a Black man and a White woman holding hands.

* * *

I spent 2 summers in high school doing volunteer work in parishes in Chicago's inner city, first at a day camp at St. Cecilia's, then living at St. James parish in a program developed by the Sisters of Mercy and tutoring children in their homes in the projects. Our stay at St. James was cut short by a week when the race riots of 1967 erupted across the country, including on Chicago's South side. A group of us sat on the front porch of St. James one evening at dusk. Michigan Avenue was eerily quiet, and sirens wailed not far off in the distance. A police car pulled over and told us to go inside, the rioting was spreading. The next day, all of us who were volunteers were sent home.

Incensed by the violence directed against Martin Luther King and the civil rights marchers who marched to Marquette Park a few miles from our homes in 1968, a friend of mine and I wrote the following letter to the editor at the Chicago newspaper *America*:

> As a comment on the March 27 article in your paper concerning the women who are picketing the schools involved in the busing program, we'd like to pose a few questions not only to those who picket but also to those who tolerate and condone this:
>
> Are not all men equal, or is there something about people who happen to have black skin that will in some way plague those of us who come in contact with them?
>
> Are not all American citizens entitled to the best possible means for a good life, including education?
>
> Are the actions of these women going to teach their children to love, or do their children only have to learn to love people with white skin?
>
> Are the actions of these women not going to turn these Negro children's love into hate for the white man?
>
> Was it not the white man who originally deprived and has continued to deprive the Negro of his sense of pride, identity, and respect that is now causing so many problems?
>
> If the wisdom that comes with age is the kind of wisdom these women seem to have acquired over the years, we hope we never grow old!
>
> Noreen Jordan
> Therese Ragen
> St. Mary's College
> Notre Dame, Indiana

The letter was published. After my father died, my mother found a folder in his filing cabinet that had a dozen Xeroxed copies of the letter as it was printed in the newspaper.

This response to our letter was published a few days later:

In answer to Noreen Jordan and Therese Ragen in regards to mothers who are picketing schools, they are correct in one thing. All American citizens are entitled to the best possible life including education—and that's why we picket.

If these two young women would find out what is going on in these schools, they might not be so quick to condemn.

It is not a racial issue. Our children also have the right to the best possible education instead of becoming full time art students. Math classes have gone back as many as 40 pages, all progressive reading groups have been discontinued in the eight receiving schools, and contrary to the board of education's figures, the class sizes have gone up, not down.

We, too, want our children to be able to go to a fine college such as St. Mary's but, if they are not allowed to learn and have the proper foundation, they will be lucky to finish high school.

I truly hope these two young women never march in a picket line to fight for the education of their children. I don't enjoy doing it myself, but someone has to fight it here and now or all children are going to suffer.

I don't march in the picket line because I claim the wisdom of the ages, but because I believe it is more important for all children to be educated than integrated.

The money spent on busing could be spent to build schools. More schools and more teachers would mean a better education for all.

I can't say I examined my underlying or unconscious prejudices and projections—I don't know that the idea of that had even been articulated in those days—but I can say I adamantly believed that prejudice and discrimination were wrong and the inequities among races were unjust and required redressing.

In my early 20s, I taught in an all-Black Catholic girls' high school. When I left there to teach in what was a predominantly White, middle-class and upper-middle-class, heavily Irish Catholic school where I had gone to high school, a friend and coteacher, also an alumna, and I went to the principal with a proposal to actively reach out beyond the usual geographical area students came from and create a multiethnic, multiracial school. The principal listened with seeming enthusiasm to her two former students and said it was a fantastic idea, but unfortunately "unrealistic."

I got my Ph.D. at Adelphi University, where the dean, Gordon Derner, was committed to having an ethnically and racially diverse group of students. After going to an Adelphi party one night with me when he was in town visiting me, my brother Tom commented that it was like being at the United Nations. At the party a friend who was talking to a new student called to me, saying he wanted to introduce us. The new student was a Black man from Chicago, who asked me what is typically one of the first questions native Chicagoans ask one another.

"What side of the city are you from?" he asked.

"The South side," I said.

"You're not from the South side," he said. "You're from the Southwest side."

I was angry and said, "I'm from the South side." It was only later I wished I'd said, "I take it you're from the Southeast side."

Despite the diversity of the doctoral program at Adelphi, the field of clinical psychology ushered me ever increasingly into a White world. My placements were all in White middle-class and upper-middle-class locations—the Farmingdale school district on Long Island, the child psychotherapy center at Long Island Jewish Hospital, the student clinic at Adelphi, and New York Hospital–Cornell Medical Center in White Plains. I didn't make any deliberate choices to change the trajectory of my career, and my continued studies in psychoanalysis only deepened it. When Harold came to see me, he was one of the few Black patients I had worked with in psychotherapy over the years.

* * *

Mary Mac wore her green uniform dress with breasts sagging down to her stomach until it was time to leave our house, then she put her bra back on, her skirt and blouse, and her stockings and high heels, and walked out the back door to wait with the other Black women who worked in the neighborhood to get the bus at 103rd and Longwood Drive. I remember one day when I was 11 or 12 hearing the back door shut and watching her walk down the hill, realizing with a sinking feeling that she always used the back door. All the other adults who came to our house used the front door. I felt sad, and then I felt an unwanted, unbidden twinge of superiority, of richness.

Sometimes Mac, Mary Mac's husband, picked up Mary Mac from work in his big, late-model black sedan. We called adults Mr. and Mrs. But not Mary Mac or Mac. We didn't call them Mrs. and Mr. MacAfee, their full names. We called them Mary Mac and Mac. As I think back over the names of the various people who worked in our house and those of friends and neighbors, I realize it was only the married White women we called by title.

I worried about how much money Mary Mac was paid, and didn't understand why all adults who worked weren't paid the same amount per hour. Overhearing a conversation between my parents one day, I learned that my parents paid her health insurance and was glad that they did.

Mary Mac's daughter and granddaughter lived with her and Mac. Mary talked about her granddaughter, Vicky, all the time. Once in a while, when Mac came to pick up Mary, Vicky would be with him. Years later when Mary Mac died, my brothers Bill and Tim and I went to the wake. As soon as we walked in Vicky came up to us, called us each by name, and hugged us. I was stunned she knew which ones out of the eight siblings in our family we were and asked her how she knew. She said her grandmother kept pictures of all of us underneath the glass on her dresser.

Before Mary Mac, Annie Price worked for my parents. She and I used to walk to Van Laten's farm stand from our apartment at 100th and Bell. It was a four- or five-block walk. On the corner of 100th and Oakley, there was a concrete block about 3 feet by 3 feet wide that we used to sit on. It stood on a concrete base about a half-foot high. We'd step up on the base and then Annie Price would pull me up onto the stoop, where she sat and put me on her lap. She sang spirituals about Jesus as Savior and her belly rose up and down as she sang, her voice low but impassioned.

When it was time to go, she'd take my hand and we'd walk the last block to Van Laten's and pick out fresh tomatoes and lettuce and corn on the cob, and carrots and peaches and plums. We'd take them up to the counter and Mrs. Van Laten would take her pencil out from behind her ear, adding up the prices in a column on a paper bag. Then Annie would take out her leather change purse and pull out the $10 bill my mother had given her and give her our address to deliver our fruit and vegetables and we'd begin the walk home again. We'd always sat so long on the way to Van Laten's we never had time to stop and sit on the concrete stoop on the way home. I'd always ask, though, and Annie Price would say, "Next time, baby. Next time."

Reggie, another African American woman, worked for my grandmother. She worked for her for years. When we moved from our apartment on Bell Avenue to a house on 102nd Street, Reggie started coming to our house every other Wednesday. She did the heavy housework. That meant twice a month Reggie came and moved the couches and chairs and tables and vacuumed underneath them. She used a thick white cream from a tin and cleaned all the wood furniture with it.

Again I feel an upsurge of some superior feeling that I am letting everyone know I am from a family that had money, and I feel guilty—guilty about the fact of it and guilty about feeling superior, feeling "look at me" about it, and I remember my mother saying my grandfather used to say to her and her brothers, "Don't ever think you're better than anyone else." He had money during the Depression when many people didn't. A lot of their extended family came and stayed from time to time with them, and he told his children to never think they were better than anyone else.

For some reason, perhaps because of Uncle Frank, though I had no conscious knowledge then of what he'd done, as a young child I had a strong sense of the inequities between White people and Black people and of the unfairness and injustice of it. For several years from about the time I was 7, my mother and grandmother, Nana, used to take my three sisters, Mary, Anne, and Katie, and me downtown on the Rock Island Railroad to shop and have lunch in the Walnut Room at Marshall Field's on State Street. We got on the train just down the street from my grandmother's at 103rd Street, and my three sisters and I would flip the back of the woven seats to make a set of seats facing each other. Pass-

ing 51st Street we saw the dome of St. Elizabeth's Church, where Nana
had been the organist as a young woman. Depending on which way
the wind was blowing, the stench from the stockyards filled the car as
we passed the area known as "Back of the Yards." When the train got
closer to downtown the neighborhoods changed from White to Black,
and the further we got the poorer the neighborhoods became. I remember staring out the open train window oblivious to everything but what
I was seeing—the small frame houses, many in states of deterioration,
sheets and towels and clothes flapping in the breeze on clotheslines hung
behind houses, Black children playing in small backyards and adults
sitting on porches.

When I was 12, the federal housing project called the Robert Taylor
Homes, recently demolished but at one time the largest housing project
in the nation, was built—16 stories, plain rectangles with thousands of
small windows, red and yellow buildings that all looked the same, set at
angles to each other on a 2-block by 2-mile stretch of land. They loomed
over the Dan Ryan Expressway. Each time we drove down the Dan
Ryan, we passed them. I remember wondering how we could all simply
drive by these buildings knowing the people living in them had so little
materially while so many of the rest of us had so much.

Now when I think about the Robert Taylor Homes I think about
Frantz Fanon's (1963) early book *The Wretched of the Earth* on the
social and psychological dynamics of the colonizer and the colonized.
These dynamics could only have been magnified in such a closed, insu-
lar, and densely populated setting as the Robert Taylor Homes. Fanon,
a psychiatrist from Martinique, discussed violence as both a means
of liberation and a catharsis to subjugation. He stated, "The 'thing'
colonized becomes a man through the very process of liberation," and
"the naked violence of colonialism only gives in when confronted with
greater violence" (p. 23). Violence, Fanon held, "is a cleansing force.
It rids the colonized of their inferiority complex, of their passive and
despairing attitude. It emboldens them, and restores their self-confi-
dence" (p. 51).

In contemporary psychoanalysis we place great emphasis on the
need for patients to enact in the treatment with their analyst that
which has been too unbearable to carry consciously. There is a lot
of discussion about how it is also inevitable that we as analysts get
caught up in our own enactments with patients, enacting split-off

parts of our self. What about the repressed or dissociated violence of the colonized, of the Black person in a White world, the violence of Harold? And what about the repressed or dissociated violence of the colonizer, the violence of the White person toward Black persons, my violence toward Harold? Well beyond frustration and anger, was there room for recognition and expression of this violence in the treatment?

Reading Fanon led me to think back on my work with Harold. There had been moments when, in sitting across from Harold, an image of my uncle would dart through my head. He was red in the face, hot and sweaty and close-up, screaming hatred pouring out of his face. With the image came a trace of the feeling of exhilaration in my body. I went back and reread the description of my uncle in *Race Riots* (Tuttle, 1996) in order to let myself see where that fleeting image and feeling would go if I allowed it fuller play.

"Throwing rocks, bricks ... storming through the front doors, smashing furniture and throwing it through windows, and putting the torch to everything"—the words pulled me in, tapping my momentary identification with Frank Ragen (Tuttle, 1996, p. 55). I had a very focused, clear feeling of exhilaration, imagining myself throwing rocks, smashing furniture, throwing it out of windows, and torching the place I'd trashed. I knew that part of me would love to do that. The repugnance and recoiling from the very idea of it then crept in, but not before I had let myself go into imagined violence and felt the thrill of that.

The notion that we are all racists took on a meaning that had flesh and blood. What of the shame and horror and outrage I had felt before about what Frank had done? They are all still there, too. Neither set of feelings exclusively holds my truth.

* * *

Harold terminated with me because of my evident chronic frustration with him. I'm embarrassed to say that he said sometimes I even rolled my eyes at what he said. He was the most frustrating person with whom I ever worked. I'd see an opening with him that, when I approached it, he'd shut down tightly. Over and over again it happened. I remember few responses Harold gave to an interpretation or an empathic remark from me that Harold didn't at least partially negate. We talked about it.

He was frustrated, too. He experienced my frustration as a criticism of him, as well he would.

We met twice a week for almost 3 years. I admired the way he terminated. Once he made the decision he didn't waver from it, but he was willing to give us some closing sessions and not terminate abruptly.

When Harold quit treatment, he was in the midst of losing his job. That was one source of my frustration. I hadn't been able to help him in a way that eased his poor relationships at work. Little by little, he was for all intents and purposes shut out of the group of stockbrokers with whom he worked.

* * *

Harold was brought up Baptist but practiced as an Episcopalian in his adult life. One of the reasons Harold was referred to me was because he had a strong and active spiritual life, which the referring psychologist thought would make for a good fit with me. I think about how little Harold and I talked about the role of the spiritual in his life. And then I think, what did we talk about?

I remember being confused a lot with Harold. I was confused by his train of thought. I was often unsure whether he was actually moving toward something or moving away from something. When I'd try to ask him about it, he always said he was moving toward something, so I should not interrupt. Then we'd get far into the session, and from what I could see he had only moved horizontally across topics, not more deeply into anything.

* * *

Judith White (2007) maintains that through the psychoanalytic process, a person of color can move away from accepting, consciously and unconsciously, an internalized devalued identity; unlearn it; and come to feel equal to White people. Similarly, she says, psychoanalysis can help a White person move from the denial of their conscious and unconscious feelings of White privilege to a positive regard for being White without feeling superior but, rather, equal to people of color.

I am at my writing desk and open the blinds to see more and let more light into the room. From my desk I have an unbelievable view of the Triborough Bridge, and what is known as Hell's Gate, the confluence of the Harlem and East Rivers. The crosscurrents are deep and dangerous. In earlier days many boats went down there. The patterns the crosscurrents make on the surface of the water are ever changing.

Lately, as I've worked on writing this piece, I've felt the impulse to write Harold and ask him to come back into treatment. I won't do that, but part of me would like to. I'd like to think we'd do the work better now.

6 Success

The Ferenczi course at the NYU Postdoctoral Program in Psychother-apy and Psychoanalysis postdoc had opened up, and I was mulling over the idea of submitting a proposal to teach it when one day on the street I bumped into the chair of the committee making the selection. We chatted briefly, and then I found myself asking how someone who was interested in teaching the course would go about applying for it. "Is it you?" he asked. I felt myself blush and told him I was thinking about it and asked if he thought it would be preposterous of me to do. He said, "No, it wouldn't be preposterous. It would be a long shot, though. You know the other person applying for it has been out of the program longer than you; he's already supervising postdoc candidates. But go for it."

In order to apply, I needed to send the faculty selection committee a letter of interest, my CV, the names of 12 former students as recom-mendations, along with a course proposal and syllabus. Preparing the proposal and syllabus took an enormous amount of work. In the middle of working on it, I received an announcement about an upcoming inter-national Ferenczi conference that was being held in Rome the following summer. It turned out the other applicant would be a speaker at it. A few days later I learned a paper he'd written on Ferenczi was about to be published in the journal *Psychoanalytic Dialogues*.

After a meeting one night, I told the chair I was thinking of with-drawing my name from consideration. He encouraged me to keep it in, saying, "That way people will know you're interested in teaching when another course opens up. And, you never know what's going to happen with this kind of thing."

So I finished the proposal and syllabus and sent them in. The next step was for the other applicant and me to teach a sample mini-class at a faculty selection committee meeting. I spent the day of the meeting rehearsing over and over what I was going to say. It was already March, but I was freezing. Two pairs of wool socks and an Irish knit sweater my mother had bought me in Ireland years ago didn't keep me warm.

My presentation started out going well. A few minutes into it I could see the minds of the committee members working, engaged by what I was presenting. I got into a kind of state of flow, my anxiety dropping away. But then toward the end of the question-and-answer period, one of the members asked me how Ferenczi had influenced my clinical work. I answered the question, but apparently not to her satisfaction. She asked again. I was missing something she was looking for, but I didn't know what it was. I stumbled a bit, and said that more than any of the particulars of his clinical technique, it is Ferenczi's spirit that has affected how I work—aspiring to his openness, creativity, concern for his patients, and willingness to explore and experiment, and the deep empathy he displayed. I couldn't tell whether or not that response satisfied the committee and left feeling a bit off center. By the time I got home, I thought I'd blown it.

In the middle of the selection process the other applicant, whom I had never met, and I wound up at a party at the Pen and Brush Club. We were called to come and listen to the hosts' daughter, an opera singer, sing an aria. I walked over with a friend to where a group was forming, and only when we were standing still did I realize I was standing directly behind him. He is a short man and I am a tall woman wearing 2-inch heels, so I looked directly down on his curly black hair. I thought of how it would not be long before the committee met and we heard which one of us will be chosen, and I stood taller, confident in that moment that my proposal would be accepted.

* * *

I received the call from the chairperson telling me I was chosen to teach the course. The faculty selection committee had recommended me, and the executive committee of the relational track approved the recommendation. That night I dreamed:

> I was in a store trying on clothes. I was trying on a green dress. A man was helping me. I was standing looking in the mirror trying to decide whether or not to buy the dress. It looked great on me, but I was worried it looked too revealing or too sexy. I was also concerned about the price and looked at the price tag again. The dress was $190. I thought it's not that expensive, but also that things add up.
>
> Then I was in a room at a retreat center where a group was meeting with Irene Dugan, a Religious of the Cenacle whom I used to see for spiritual direction. Irene, vocal and direct but very caring, worked doing spiritual direction and retreats, despite the fact that she was unable to walk the last several years of her life and got around in an electric wheelchair until she died at age 86. The group that was meeting with Irene was at a round table. I looked for a seat. It looked like the only one left was next to her, but then I saw that it had a notebook on it, indicating it was saved like a lot of the other places did. I said I thought we were one seat short. Irene said actually there were a lot more people coming. They set up more tables, and I was way down at the end and there was an office partition blocking my view. I felt horrible, very depressed then, because I had thought Irene would be able to tell me whether I should buy the dress or not, whether or not I looked good in it and okay in it, and now I wouldn't be able to ask her. I was too far away. I thought of how I would stay at the retreat center after the meeting and try to deal with how depressed I felt and how I'd be the only one left; everyone else would be gone. I saw nuns in the old full black habit walking off in the distance.

As I got up out of bed, I thought about what I would wear to work and remembered I'd gone shopping the past weekend, and the thought came, "You should take all those clothes back. You should return them."

I was at the Vinegar Factory getting a bagel for breakfast. I saw one in the bin I liked and heard this voice in my head saying, "Then you shouldn't have that one."

The dream stayed with me throughout the day. I thought about what Irene represents—the power and competence, the independence and freedom, of nuns' lives as I saw it growing up. They were women who were sovereign over their own domains, whether it was a school, hospital, or retreat center. The other group of women I grew up seeing were the women in the neighborhood, an area called Beverly on the South side of Chicago. Beverly was largely an Irish Catholic neighborhood where the women did not have to work outside the home to make ends meet. People had large families. The women stayed home raising the children, and the men were professionals or businessmen. At that time, women in the Catholic Church would ask the priest in confession how long they could use rhythm after giving birth. It was a time, as my mother said, when she "and a lot of women just went along and accepted and adjusted to whatever happened—like it or not."

My mother and I saw the production *Contact* a few years ago on a trip she made to New York. In a scene in which a man is belittling and berating his wife during dinner at a restaurant, my mother turned to me and said, "She ought to knock the table over onto him—but she can't, it's the 50s." That same weekend at the Museum of Modern Art (MOMA), we saw the Picasso painting *Three Women at a Spring* of large-boned, full, strong women. Their arms and hands were massive. My mother stood in front of it for a long time, and then, lifting her forearms and making fists with both of her hands, she said, "It's wonderful to see such strong women beautifully portrayed, isn't it?"

* * *

My mother left college when her father died. It was during World War II, and her three brothers were in the service. She returned home from St. Mary's of Notre Dame to live with her mother so she wouldn't be alone. When my youngest brother, the youngest of eight, went to first grade, my mother went to St. Xavier's College to finish her college education. In my office file cabinet is a manila folder marked "Mom's papers," which includes a psychology paper and a theology paper my mother wrote when she returned to college. I read them when she wrote them in 1968 and asked if I could have them. It had been years since I looked at them, and recently I dug them out. The theology paper dealt with the immanence versus the transcendence of God. The psychology paper was a review of Karen Horney's book *The Neurotic Personality of Our Time* (1937). In it my mother wrote,

> Perhaps Karen Horney would analyze it as wishful thinking on my part but I fail to see the contradiction she places between competition and success on the one hand and brotherly love and humility on the other. She states that within the normal range you must take one seriously and discard the other or take both seriously with the result that the individual is seriously inhibited in both directions. I don't think it's necessarily neurotic to compete and be successful and at the same time accept Christian ideals. For many people these ideals are the very thing that makes life in this competitive world easier to bear. Possibly this would be construed as "selling out" to the young, but it is making an adjustment and Miss Horney indicates that this is what the neurotic cannot do, while the normal person can.

* * *

At dinner one night with my niece Therese, I got a look at how the next generation in my family saw the culture my siblings and I grew up in. Therese was talking about her mother, my sister Anne, and how she is looking at her life and what to do next now that her youngest child will be going to college. Therese's voice began to crack. I asked, "What is it that's touching you so much?"

She said, "That it was all or none for you and my mom. My dad got to have a family and his career because my mom focused all her attention on raising us. And when Aunt Katie [my youngest sister] became an adult, she was in a group of women who could have both a career and a family. And for Aunt Mary [my oldest sister] and her friends, it wasn't even a question—not for South side, middle-class, upper-middle-class Irish Catholic girls in Chicago. But for you and my mom you had a choice, only it was all or none."

I couldn't talk through the lump in my throat but nodded my head vigorously. I took all and I took none, and my sister Anne, 18 months younger, took all and took none. She is 51, the youngest of her five children leaves home next year, her 30th wedding anniversary is next week, her husband is vice president of a large international company, and they live in a four-bedroom home in Lake Forest. I'm 52 and about to begin teaching in the Postdoctoral Program at NYU. I've had four essays accepted for publication in the last year, have a full private practice, and live alone in a one-bedroom apartment in New York City.

* * *

The afternoon after I received word I had been chosen to teach the Ferenczi course, I lay down on the couch in my office to take a nap. My mind returned to the dream of the man helping me in the store. Then an image of me in some childhood home movies comes to mind. My sisters and brothers and other kids from the neighborhood were in our back-yard. The image I saw of me was of a pretty, calm, thin girl standing in line at the picnic table waiting to get a piece of cake. Her shoulders and arms are pretty in the sundress she was wearing. She looked calm and poised and self-possessed and at peace. I remember how struck I was by the image when I saw those movies for the first time again as an adult, how surprised that that was me—not a wild or rambunctious, active kid who was in constant motion with a gleam in her eye. I lay there moving into that image of myself, reclaiming it, getting to know it, feeling the comfort and femininity and peacefulness, the self-knowledge of it. She looked like a child who knew who she was and who was comfortable in her own skin.

I entered into a kind of reverie, a half-waking half-sleeping state, and then dozed off. I dreamed of myself as a girl, the same age as I was in the movies—5, maybe 6 years old. I was sitting on the floor up against the wall in some kind of contraption in which there's a curved black metal bar protruding out over me. My head was down, my hair disheveled and hanging in front of my face, covering it, and then a gun came into the front of the picture and was pointed down at my head, and I heard the man holding the gun say to another man with him, "She knows too much," and I woke in terror.

* * *

Within minutes of getting the phone call that I had gotten the course, I had the unbidden thought, "They'll kill you."

"Who?" I asked myself and saw the photograph of the truck from which the Mafia gunmen shot my grandfather, and a splitting, tingling, numbing, dizzying sensation spread through my head.

Just the night before, I had looked at newspaper clippings about my grandfather's shooting for a piece I was thinking about writing about him. Opening the yellow pages, torn in pieces at their folds, I saw a photograph of the truck the gunmen had used. The police discovered it abandoned on the street at 43rd and Union on the South side of Chicago. The accompanying story revealed it had been stolen 3 months earlier from an H. Finchhammer in Benton Harbor, Michigan. It was a black pickup truck with shining silver grillwork and trim, and a tarp extending over the back open section of it, the tarp that went up when the truck pulled up next to Grandpa's car the day before, riddling his car with bullets. There was a lengthy article beginning on the front page of the paper—the June 25, 1946, *Chicago Herald American*—explaining how the Mafia had wanted my grandfather to sell them his racing news information business, which consisted of Continental Wire Service and the *Green Sheet*, and he refused.

On page 1, there was a photograph of Grandpa taken some time before he was shot. It's a close-up of him. He was wearing a suit and tie and wire-rim glasses. His round face looked soft, his eyes intent. I thought of a friend of the family once telling me my grandfather was the gentlest man she'd ever met. The caption under the photograph read, "Gangland Barrage Cuts Down Race News Magnate."

I turned over the page and looked again at the photo of the truck. In the background was a crowd of people from the neighborhood looking at the truck and at the reporters taking pictures. Behind them was a row of Chicago brick bungalows.

I had just heard I was selected for the postdoc faculty, and in my mind's eye I see the truck the gunmen used to shoot my grandfather. And still, I am elated. The image and the feeling sit side by side, occurring simultaneously but disconnected, like a split screen.

The split screen unfolds into an image of my friend, Debbie Gold, and me together at a Bar Mitzvah. As the image unfolds, Debbie, her 6-year-old daughter Lili, and I are holding hands, forming a circle and doing the hora. Some people were clapping their hands over their heads. Others were dancing in circles within circles. Lili and Debbie and I spun round together. More people flooded onto the floor, and the music and clapping and dancing were deafening, and I picked up Lili and twirled her around. Minutes earlier, she had asked me what my Hebrew name was, and I said I didn't have one and she and Debbie decided to give me one. Debbie thought the Hebrew word for "goodness" or maybe "truth." In the midst of somberly thinking, Lili's eyes brightened, and she said, "No. No. I know what it is." Then, softly, "Beauty. Her name is Be-a-u-u-tee," she said, stretching the "u" of *Beauty*.

"Twirl me faster, Be-a-u-u-tee!" she called back to me then, and I saw myself twirling Lili as fast as I could go, her dangling legs flying through the air, her red velvet dress soft in my arms.

I saw myself twirling her like a skater spinning on ice, our dance becoming a blur of Lili's red dress. She was shrieking in delight, the band was playing faster, and I was spinning with abandon, not knowing where I was going, spinning across the now cleared floor. Three men with submachine guns walked toward the dance floor. I released Lili, told her to run, and stretched my arms out flying through the air, calling, "Faster! Still faster!" to the band.

7 Kate

Kate has cancer. She left a message earlier today, saying she was going to call on the phone rather than come into the office for our Wednesday 6:00 p.m. appointment. When we talked she told me she had begun having trouble swallowing late last week, and her doctor had discovered a tumor on her esophagus. She was unable to swallow any food because of the obstruction of the tumor. They had performed surgery 2 days earlier to insert a feeding tube into Kate's body.

They had done a CAT scan and MRI, and were going to begin treatment immediately, both chemotherapy and radiation. Her oncologist told her to call her children and tell them. He said there was little hope that Kate would live.

Kate dreaded calling her three grown children with this news. She cried softly as she talked to me about how unimaginable it was that she would have to tell them she had cancer and would likely die. She didn't want them to have to bear this, and she thought telling them would make it real not only to them but to herself as well.

I slumped in my chair at the other end of the line, stunned at the news and heavyhearted for her. I listened closely, doing the only thing I knew how to do at the moment—I was simply present, quiet, with her.

As I walked through the Union Square subway station to get the train home, Kate was on my mind. After the call I found myself feeling buoyant, liberated somehow, which was perplexing. I felt a deep feeling of generosity toward Kate, freed somehow to be closer and more giving. It felt backwards to me, a reaction of someone who was out of touch with herself. Reflecting on this on my trip home, I realized that I felt safe with Kate in a way I had not before then. In her fear and sadness, I felt safe to give to her, more confident she would accept any tenderness I might offer. Was it that the prospect of Kate's death freed me from my own fears about intimacy—that I could get closer to her now because if she was dying I didn't have to be worried about being swallowed up or overwhelmed in the closeness? Was I in a kind of hypomanic state, denying the possibility of her dying?

* * *

My father died of Alzheimer's 13 years after he was diagnosed with it. I was in Chicago for my niece Therese's wedding and standing at the front door of my parents' home, my suitcase in one hand, the key to the rental car in my other, when the phone rang. It was the hospice worker from the nursing home calling my mother to say that it might be a few hours or it might be a few days, but my father was dying. Within an hour of the call all of us, except my brother Joe in California, were gathered in my dad's room in the nursing home—my mother, 6 of my brothers and sisters, their spouses, myself, and 15 of the older grandchildren.

We enveloped him, my mother, and each other in our love. We sang my father's alma mater for him, "Notre Dame, Our Mother" and the "Notre Dame Fight Song." My mother led us in the rosary. That night my mother and most of my siblings and I stayed at the nursing home, spelling each other so someone was always with my father. The next morning he died, with us again gathered around him in his bed.

My father's death was for me such an experience of freely and deeply being loved and loving. Is this what led me to the newly freed feeling of love and generosity with Kate?

* * *

Kate first came to see me 4 years earlier. She said she felt like she was in a rut, or, as she put it once, that she was like a billiard ball bouncing off of one thing and then another, without a sense of purpose or direction. She was curious and intelligent. When she talked about something that captured her attention, whether a book, a play, the places to which she traveled, or the high school students to whom she taught history, she came to life, a vivacious and energetic woman. But her baseline state was much flatter, like she was worn out. She was looking within and without for something or someone who would spark her enthusiasm for life.

Kate and I liked each other, but there was an uneasy tension that permeated our work. At the end of the first session, when I told her my fee she burst out with "Wow! You must think you're really something!" Months later, when she discovered from talking with friends what psychologists' fees generally were in Manhattan, she apologized. But it was the kind of sarcasm she often used, and I felt on guard with her.

With some regularity, we asked ourselves what we were doing, whether we were getting anywhere in the treatment. We enjoyed each other, our senses of humor playing off of each other. I felt guilty about that sometimes and hoped the work was taking place in and through our senses of humor.

Kate was a feeling, sensitive person but filled with shame that stopped her from going forward at the first hint of vulnerability. Time after time in our sessions, when she had a strong feeling, she would go into an emotional lockdown. Many times each session I would have to ask Kate to speak up because she spoke so low. She sat at the far end of the couch and I'd move my chair closer to her, but still had to ask her to speak louder.

* * *

Kate called. She began with a strong "hello" and said she was having a good week. She said her energy was coming back and she felt so well it was hard for her to realize how sick she actually is.

"Every day," she said, "I open my eyes and say, 'Okay, I've got another one.' I feel like I'm on a wonderful spiritual journey."

She had gone to Graymoor, a Catholic retreat center, and on the way there the friend she was with told her about a workshop she'd attended on Teresa of Avila and Therese of Lisieux. Later in the day, sitting by the river, her friend asked if she would like to do a guided meditation exercise she'd learned. The exercise took Kate into a castle, Teresa of Avila's metaphor of the soul. In each room something different happened. In the first room she was to open a heavy door, and, once inside the room, call in the person she knew loved her unconditionally, and go and sit next to that person, just absorbing that person's love. To her surprise, she called in her father, with whom she had locked horns throughout her life, rather than her mother, whom she adored. She said she thought to herself, "Do I have this so wrong?"

"Sometimes," she said, "I feel like I'm floating and I ask myself, 'Is this my chance at a life I should have been living?' I just keep having one lovely thought that leads to another. There are so many strong, wise, loving people in my life. Sometimes I think I have to be careful, like I'm too happy and then I ask myself, 'What am I? Nuts?'"

* * *

Every time I wrote about Kate my throat began to ache. The longer I wrote the more it would ache, and when I stopped writing the ache would fade away.

* * *

In the following session, also on the phone, Kate told me about having seen an oncologist who specialized in treating cancer with supplementary techniques—homeopathy, yoga, diet, and exercise. He told her he was hopeful his regimen would cure her cancer. That session I felt very present to her again. I noticed her voice sounded differently now. It was louder and lighter, more full of life. She sounded open and vulnerable, and that enkindled feelings of openness and vulnerability in me.

It was only in this new experience of her and each other that I realized just how on edge I had felt with her. Before, when I tried to talk to her about the hostility in her sarcasm, she would say I was too sensitive and put the problem back on me, and I would feel defensive. That session I had the thought that if she was sarcastic I could stay open enough to her to talk about it in a way that she could hear and that might lead us someplace new. Perhaps we would get to the pain buried under the sarcasm.

I keep thinking about the threat of loss and the openness and vulnerability to which it leads. Why do we live more closed off from ourselves and one another when we are not facing loss? What is it we are anxious about such that we live our daily lives so defensively? Specifically, what about the openness, the vulnerability, and the intimacy frightens us in our day-to day-living yet does not frighten us in the face of loss?

Is it our fear of merger? Are we afraid if we get too close to others that we will lose our sense of ourselves as separate, individuated, autonomous persons? Why does the threat of death free us from these fears?

Is it because with the prospect of death we know there will be an end to the closeness, that death will keep us from losing ourselves in merger?

Why, too, do we not learn from our experiences of loss or near loss? We don't, in fact, fuse with others. What keeps us from taking that knowledge back to our lives and allowing it to free us to more openness and vulnerability and intimacy?

* * *

Shortly into the following session Kate said, "I don't want to be Superwoman. My doctor told me, 'If anyone can kick ass through this treatment, you can.' But I don't want to always be strong. Sometimes I'm just a wimp."

Kate had gone to get a wig, something she'd put off for days. She said she couldn't even put it on, and she left it in the bag from the store. She felt embarrassed by the idea of wearing a wig. Seeing her scalp "unglued" her, she said. One night she woke in the middle of the night and had the thought of coming to see me in her wig, and she began to cry.

Kate had barely spoken to anyone about her worries, her fears of illness and death. She's feeling fine physically, but the fears she holds back shadow her. She's not afraid of the fact of dying. She said it would be fine if she could pass out quietly on her back porch. It's the cancer metastasizing, the needles, surgery, the IVs, that terrify her. And the thought of her children at her hospital bed saddens her beyond words.

On the one hand, it's a "lovely gesture" when friends and family bring up her cancer, giving her an opening to discuss it. But then in the middle of the conversation, she finds herself thinking, "Oh, stop this!" and doesn't want to talk about it anymore. On the other hand, she wishes she had someone to talk freely with about her fears and sadness. An old friend asked her recently how she was really feeling and Kate began to tell her. Her friend cut her off, saying, "We manifest what we think. You shouldn't think about your fears."

Kate recalled when her mother was in the hospital and her mother's brother came to visit. He was holding her hand. Her mother said she thought it was time for her to die, and he said, "Now, stop that!"

"Nobody lets you talk about death," Kate remarked. "I'm surrounded by people who won't let me express any fear or doubt. Sometimes I feel like Pollyanna."

I said it must feel lonely, and she said, yes, it did. She thought she probably needed to talk to someone about the loneliness of being so ill and figured I'd be the one. I started to say, "I'm very happy to," then corrected myself, saying, "No, I'm not happy, but I want very much for you to feel able to talk with me about your fears."

"Most of me feels I'm going to be all right," she said.

"But there's that part of you that doesn't," I said.

* * *

My first encounter with death was when my Uncle Jerry, my father's younger sister's husband, committed suicide. The image I had in my mind as a 9 year old was that Uncle Jerry had slipped on a pink throw rug in front of the dresser in a policeman friend's house while he was looking at the policeman's gun and the gun had gone off, accidentally killing him. I had some vague idea of what a wake was, and imagined Uncle Jerry propped up dead standing in a glass box. I remember the shock I felt when my friend down the block, Judy Rapp, showed me the article in the *Chicago Tribune* newspaper her mother had shown her. It was on the bottom left-hand side of the obituary pages in the paper. The headline said, "Relative of Ragen Commits Suicide." I learned in the article that Uncle Jerry had committed suicide and that my grandfather Ragen had been killed by the Mafia.

The morning Dad called to say Nana, my mother's mother, had died, I left home early enough to stop at my parents' home on the way to work. As I pulled up on the street in front of the house, my father was walking down the driveway on the way to 8:00 morning Mass. I watched him. He had tears in his eyes. I didn't understand. I wondered why he was crying; it wasn't his mother who had died. I waited until he'd passed before I got out of the car and went to the door. I rang the bell. My mother answered in her robe and nightgown. She and I sat on the green stools at the snack bar in the kitchen while she ate a bowl of shredded wheat and told me about being called and then going to the hospital in the middle of the night.

That evening my siblings and I were all at my parents' for dinner. We didn't talk during dinner about Nana's dying. Later, when I went to my cousin's house to plan the funeral Mass, my cousin broke down crying. Her mother put her arms around her and held her to herself. I had no idea what to do.

I was 23 years old when Nana died. After my mother and father married they moved into my grandmother's house with her. A few years after that, Nana bought a two-flat building. Nana lived upstairs, and my mom and dad, my older sister and brother, and I lived on the first floor. When our family grew larger, we moved into a house and Nana into an apartment building down the block.

I had never encountered death before, and it would be another 30-some years before my father died and I would experience another death in my family. Nana had cancer. The last time I visited her in her apartment, she told me how fortunate she felt to be able to stay in her apartment despite the fact she had cancer. Soon after, she was hospitalized and died a few weeks later. During the time of her hospitalization, on my frequent drives down Lake Shore Drive on the way to Passavant Hospital to visit her, I practiced over and over in my mind telling her that I loved her. I urgently felt I needed and wanted to do this. As the days passed, Nana slipped into a semicomatose state. It was a rainy November day when I finally worked up the nerve to tell her. I stood next to her bed, my hand encircling her wrist, and leaned over and in her ear said, "I love you." I had never in my life spoken those words. I was surprised by their absorption into the everyday ether. I don't know what it is I expected would happen, but something earth shattering. I also felt it was cowardly of me to wait until she was semicomatose and unable to respond, but I had been too anxious about it to do it before then.

* * *

The next session Kate talked to me about our conversation from the week before, about how isolated she felt in her frightened and sad feelings about her tumor. She told me she'd thought of calling and leaving a message during the week but never had. She said having talked about her feelings with me she slept better that night, and hadn't been conscious of feeling that alone with her fears this week.

"It's not about dwelling on the negative," she said. "It's about being able to make a space for it as a possibility without getting lectured about being negative." She added, "You're better than Chinese herbs!" We laughed.

And then she said that she was feeling really good. She had been to see "the cucumber man," as she called him. Her son had heard about this man through a coworker who recovered from cancer, and he brought

Kate to see him. The man told her that he, himself, had had inoperable lung cancer 20 years ago and was cured by the amino acids in the sea cucumbers harvested from Indonesia. He said he's an importer for Wal-Mart and he makes no money from selling the sea cucumbers. The price of the sea cucumber was $449 a month, and he said Kate would have to buy a 6-month supply to get the full benefit of it.

Her children wanted to pitch in and pay for this and the various extra treatments Kate was trying. "It's such a change," she said. "I was always the one buying things for them and helping them." We talked a bit about her allowing them to put out the amount of money it would mean. She was reluctant, especially because one son had three children and already was working extra shifts.

When Kate was in the hospital, she found herself letting her daughter "orchestrate" everything that was going on, down to what information Kate was told about her condition. Her daughter stayed with Kate for a week after she got out of the hospital. Then Kate urged her to go home, saying she'd be okay. But the day her daughter left, Kate couldn't stop crying. "I was like an 8-year-old kid whose mother says she's going to leave. It was such a deep fear," she said. "It was like the person who was keeping me safe was going and it shook me to the core. I thought to myself, 'Look how this has flipped. It was fascinating how quickly it had flipped.'"

Kate's daughter had taken her to see a healer. Kate asked me what I thought of healers. I told her I'd never been to one, but had done a lot of bodywork and found it very helpful, thinking of my back and the sustained relief I'd gotten from a particular practitioner who used a combination of naprapathy, chiropractics, and homeopathy. She said she thinks there's often something to healers.

The healer, a Chinese man named Mr. Woo, sat her down at a card table with her palms up. Kate closed her eyes and tried to be open to the experience. The man's hands hovered just over the various energy spots in her body, and he motioned like he was pulling something out of her. He said he was activating her energy centers. When he worked over her heart, she had a fit of coughing. When he moved to her spine, she began to sneeze. As his hands went over each energy center, Kate found that part of her body warming. She felt good at the end, and the Chinese man told her that her optimism and good heart and kindness as a person were giving no room for the tumor to grow or spread. She made another appointment to see him the following week.

I hadn't known it, but Kate had been practicing tai chi regularly for the past several years. She said the effect of her healing treatment was like that of her tai chi. With both she felt more of a sense of inner balance afterwards.

Kate's thinking about returning to work. The oncologist told her he wouldn't advise it because her immune system is too compromised to be around so many people. Her integrative medicine doctor said he thought it would be good for her. She's mulling it over. She has a couple of more weeks to decide.

Shortly before our session was to end, I became aware of a deep feeling of sadness inside me. When we hung up, I noticed how the small of my back ached and realized I was feeling sadness mixed with fear. I wondered where it came from, and thought back over the session. It was as though I had two different parts of myself participating in the session, and there was an inner disconnect. One part of my self was listening to the strength in Kate's voice, hearing her humor, admiring her optimism and openness, feeling with her a sense of well-being. And then there was another part of my self that throughout the conversation remembered that all of what Kate was telling me about came from the fact that she had an inoperable cancerous tumor, and I felt sad for what she was going through and afraid that she would die.

I asked myself why I hadn't become aware of feeling sad and afraid until late in the session, and worried I hadn't helped Kate be in touch with her own sadness and fear. I began to think I had joined her in a hypomanic defense against her deeper feelings. But then I asked myself why I assumed her optimism was the more superficial feeling. Perhaps it came from as deep a wellspring in her as her darker feelings.

* * *

I began to read what I could find in the psychoanalytic literature about working with patients who had life-threatening illnesses or were dying. I found a small number of contemporary articles. One theme among them was that when people have a life-threatening illness or are dying, they often come to experience a renewed sense of vitality. Positive feelings about life and about themselves intensify. This was certainly true of Kate. Facing cancer, she delighted in watching the birds from her porch and felt that she was "on a spiritual journey surrounded by love and care." Knoblauch (1995) noted that a dying patient of his, "ironically, could experience feelings and connection to others more in her dying than at any time previously in her life" (p. 212). A dying patient working with Bass (2001) "said with tears in his eyes and a smile on his face, that these few months were the best time in his life" (p. 699). Hoffman (1979), in facing his own mortality, pointed out that in confronting one's own mortality, one discovers one's "self more fully when he perceives clearly that he will die," and that "the anticipation of one's own death promotes a consolidation of self" (p. 256). Working with a patient with a life-threatening illness, Frommer (2005) wrote, "She finds herself free and able to appreciate the ongoing moments of her life in ways she has never been able to before ... being in touch with the transience of her life, is what makes her experience vibrant" (p. 497).

Other writers have remarked on the leveling effect of death on the analytic relationship itself. "Appearances, role expectations, and narcissistic hierarchies of the higher and lower shrink in importance before death the great leveler," Shabad said (2001, 703–704). My reaction to Kate during this time was similar to Adams-Silvan's (1994), who noted in her treatment of a dying woman, "I was aware that I myself felt a kind of relaxation from a long and professional accumulation of technical guidelines, experience, requirements and even strictures" (p. 338). Much like the opening that was occurring between Kate and me, Locker (2007) described how the connection opened up between her and her patients around her own mother's death:

> What began for me that first morning, with that first call, and what continued over a period of several weeks, with ongoing vibrations, has been a process of intensified connection brought about by what I like to think of as a meeting of the souls, a step beyond a meeting of minds. This was made possible only by the true "leveling of the playing field" that came about by my vulnerability, and the patients' ability to recognize and experience their own power and capacity to love. (p. 13)

* * *

As soon as I heard Kate's voice, strong and upbeat, on the phone I knew she'd gotten good news. The new CAT scan she'd had showed that the tumor had shrunk significantly. It was absolutely inoperable because of its being on the esophagus, so close to her heart and other vital organs. She will have to be on some form of chemotherapy the rest of her life if she makes it through this acute period. Her oncologist wants to give her heavy doses of chemotherapy now, to "bombard" her body with it over the next few months. It would mean 6-hour treatments of chemotherapy every 3 weeks repeated six times over. Her radiologist wants to continue radiation treatment on the tumor on her esophagus. She asked now that the tumor had shrunk what the focus of the treatment would be. Her doctor said the biggest worry was that the cancer in her lymph nodes would spread. They wanted "to go after any errant, loose cancer cells that might be floating around with the strong doses of chemotherapy."

One of Kate's friends remarked on how relaxed Kate seemed. "I know that's true," she said. "I don't know why."

When Kate went for a consultation at Sloan Kettering, she was impressed with what a beautiful building it was. I was there once when my friend Debbie was operated on for cancer. I have no recollection of what the building looked like. All I remember is the moment in the recovery room when Debbie asked her surgeon if she was going to live and he said he didn't know. That was 7 years ago, and Debbie is doing well.

At the beginning of Kate's appointment, she was instructed to put on a hospital gown. "It was so irritating," she said. "There was no need for a gown." The consultation began with a young doctor asking Kate a lot of "irritating, stupid questions." Her daughter, who had accompanied Kate, said it was a good sign that Kate was so oppositional. "You just refuse to be the sick one," she had said. Kate said, "The cancer is just not something I can dwell on because there's just no sense to it. I can't live like that."

Kate talked about how fortunate she was to have a family that was as caring as hers. She was deeply gratified by how her children were reacting to her illness. They were talking a lot among themselves, drawing closer together. Kate said, "My wish as a mother has been that these children of mine lean on one another, that they actually are a unit, and that's coming about now."

It was almost time to end, and I told Kate that I was really happy about her good news. She thanked me for telling her that, saying,

"Sometimes I forget people care, so when you say that it surprises me a little." I've thought about that moment a number of times since then, and each time I feel an almost physical opening, a sensation of softening around my heart.

* * *

A card arrived in the mail today from the New York Zen Center for Contemplative Care asking for a donation to help fund their work, much of which is with people who are dying. The card quoted a dying patient named Rose with whom center chaplains had worked in the past year. Rose said, "I've been trying to come to terms with the fact that I am going to die very soon. I never expected it to be such a joyous experience. I feel the most loving I've been in my life."

It seems to me that when I come to new understandings in life, I often then see and hear examples of those understandings that had surrounded me all along, but that I'd never really noticed. This idea of the experience of illness and death being a time of love and joy, as well as sadness and loss, is one of those new understandings for me. It was 3 years ago that my father died. Not only did our family feel grief, but I think that during that time all of us also felt held in the love of one another in a way we never had before. It still puzzles me—this opening up that comes in the face of loss, this love that unfolds.

One day, sitting in my office waiting for Kate to arrive, I found myself a bit on edge. This was to be our first session in my office, rather than on the phone, since Kate was diagnosed with cancer. I was worried that I would close up in her presence and she would close up in mine—that we would go back to the guarded, cautious way we were before. I found myself having a fleeting fantasy that Kate would walk in and make a smart remark about how short my hair was cut, but realized a moment later that we were in a different place and this was unlikely to happen. Then the doorbell rang.

I thought Kate looked good. She looked healthy. She'd lost some weight. Her wig looked like her own hair. I told her that she looked good and that her wig looked very natural.

"I hate this wig. I hate the whole idea of a wig," Kate said as she sat down. "How am I supposed to know how to handle a wig in the rain?" she added. Her daughter had to leave the restaurant where they'd just had dinner in order to go and buy an umbrella, because it had started to rain and Kate didn't know what rain would do to the wig. "It's all so stupid," she remarked.

Later, when I reflected back on the session, I was taken aback by my immediate reaction and statement to Kate that she "looked good." I realized I could only have been minimizing the gravity of Kate's illness to react in this way. My denial covered my own disturbed feelings about what was happening to Kate. She had told me that she spent great care when she was leaving the house not to look like she was a patient. In minimizing the illness she had, and its effects on her, I avoided my own feelings of powerlessness and loss, which left me unable to validate Kate's own deep reality of having a life-threatening illness.

We talked about Kate's ambivalence about returning to work. She would need to decide if she was going to go back by the time the holidays were over. That's when she would run out of sick days. She had taken the student teachers she supervised at work out for lunch to thank them for covering for her. They hadn't gotten any supervision since Kate left and were floundering without it. She wanted to go back to work with them, but dreaded working with the new principal who had recently been hired.

The more we talked, the less afraid I was that our way of relating would revert back to how it had been. There was a relaxed sense that had never been there before, at least not when we met in person. Partway through the session, Kate asked, "So, how did you imagine we'd be with each other tonight?"

I said, "Shouldn't I be the one asking that?" We chuckled with each other, and then I told her what I'd been imagining while I was sitting waiting for her. I told her that I hadn't realized until she got sick and we were talking all the time on the phone how careful and guarded I was with her.

Kate said she had mistrusted me and kept me at a distance because she was afraid I'd "pull the rug out" from under her if she got too close. She had never been sure I cared for her until she got sick, and she thought I hadn't realized how much she cared about me.

We smiled a warm, deep smile at each other from which neither of us flinched.

"It's so good to see you I could cry," Kate said.

I sat quietly in my office after Kate left, aware of the smell of incense I'd lit earlier in the day in the room, and the headache it was beginning to give me. On a glass table at the foot of my couch is a crystal vase my sister Anne gave me when I opened my first office in Chicago and a floral ceramic lamp my mother bought for me for my office. On the windowsill is the clock my friend Kathy gave me when I opened my office in New York. I sat at my dad's desk writing.

I found myself reflecting on the singularity of the therapeutic relationship. There is no other relationship like it. Anticipating Winnicott's (1967) idea of potential space, Otto Rank (1936/1945) believed that "the therapeutic situation offers the patient a plane of illusion on which not only can he live as long as he has it, but on which he can learn how to live" (p. 244). Potential space is "sacred to the individual in that it is here that the individual experiences creative living" (Winnicott, 1967, p. 372). The therapeutic relationship is both "real" and "unreal." At its best, it is a paradoxical space of emotional play that is highly personal and deeply affecting to both parties, albeit in different ways. With and through each other, Kate and I were creating an ongoing interpersonal relationship in which we were exploring and discovering new dimensions of ourselves and each other, and, by extension, what is possible in relationship. It was in the structure of that relationship that Kate could speak her fear and sadness, and expect that I would hold them with her in ways her family and friends might not be able to in the midst of their own pain.

Therapy was a place for her to express all her feelings about having cancer and possibly dying. And it was inevitable that it would be a place in which Kate would experience yet another, this time me, in denial and protest about her dying. The difference was that, unlike in other relationships, it was incumbent on me to reflect on that denial and those protests. The point of the relationship was Kate and staying present with her while not running away from the possibility of her dying.

* * *

Kate began the next session with "I buzzed my head and it feels much better. It looks weird, but the other way, with clumps of hair falling out, it looked scary. I looked like someone who was sick."

Kate had gotten a PET scan on Christmas Eve. Two nights later, she awoke from a dream, not remembering the content of it, but feeling the cancer had spread. She felt down and lethargic all day. Then her doctor called to tell her that the cancer that was in two of her lymph nodes and one adrenal gland was completely gone, and in the other of her adrenal glands it had shrunk significantly. Kate said the doctor kept saying, "This is remarkable." Kate and I laughed together in delight. I found myself saying, "Do you think it was the cucumber man?" Kate responded, "It was you, all my friends and family, the cucumber man, and Master Woo. It was this swirl of caring I've been living in, and it was the chemotherapy and the radiation." Hearing her serious response, I felt embarrassed I had been flippant, using humor in the old way we had.

Kate talked again about going back to work. She said she didn't miss it and would only go back for the money. "I dread all the attention of people's welcome backs," she said. "I hate all that attention."

Kate was going to the acupuncturist on a weekly basis now and had begun to let her insert the acupuncture needles into her body. "I took my wig off last week," she said, "and that crazy woman put needles in my head!"

Then Kate said she wanted to talk about her relationship with me. She recalled, "I wanted to have an intimate relationship and thought I'd practice on you. But I had no idea you can have that kind of relationship in therapy." She continued, "Loving someone is the easy part. It's letting yourself be loved that is the hard part. There is no relationship, no intimacy, without that. What was missing was I wasn't expecting anything from you. It just seemed like maybe when this cancer hit, I needed you to care and maybe I let you care about me."

I was deeply touched by Kate's insight and felt joyful about it with her. I mainly just sat with what she was saying. I thought about telling her about how it was different for me now, too, with her. We both were letting ourselves be loved and vulnerable, and it was hard to parse out each of our roles in it. We were in what the early 20th-century psychoanalyst Melanie Klein (1984) referred to as "the benign circle" of love (p. 131). It was being created mutually between us, but this was Kate's therapy, this was her liberating insight into herself, and I didn't think my part in it belonged in this moment. That was for another time. I simply told her that I thought the opening that was occurring in our relationship was incredible. "It's great, and I love it," I said to her.

As we were ending, Kate said she hoped she'd be able to make it into the office in person for our next session. She asked if I had another appointment following hers next week. I told her that I didn't and asked what she was wondering about. She said, "Oh, it's really nice to think of being the only one. It goes with the territory of feeling closer. It doesn't make any sense. I know your appointment book is full, but I like my fantasy that this is a very special and unique relationship and there's no one coming after me."

* * *

Kate called again today instead of coming into the office. She was tired and planning to go to sleep after we finished our session. She had started her new treatment plan and had been through 6 hours of chemotherapy today, which was to be repeated in 3 weeks. She had been apprehensive about the side effects it might bring on, but, so far, she was feeling okay, just very tired. The session consisted mainly in Kate telling me the story of her week. It had been unsettling to her to switch to a new chemotherapy unit run by different nurses and left her with a sense of loss about the nurses she'd grown to know and like. She had decided to try to go back to work next week and see what it was like. She asked if I'd had a good New Year's holiday, and I told her I'd been skiing in upstate New York. She told me she has plans to ski at Butternut in Massachusetts in February. We talked some about our mutual love of skiing and how we both found it important to ski at least once a year. "Otherwise," as Kate put it, "you wind up being a person who doesn't ski anymore."

Kate told me she had gotten a piece of food lodged in her esophagus on the day of New Year's Eve. She called her doctor, who said she would call the hospital and have an operating room prepared. She would have to do surgery on Kate to remove the food. Then, as Kate was getting dressed to go, the food dislodged on its own when she raised her arms above her head. Kate went on to entertain the company she had invited over and had "a magnificent time."

Later, thinking about the session, what struck me was that it wasn't the kind of session anyone writes about. It wasn't replete with turmoil, conflict, or intense emotion. The tone of it was one of ease between us. It was a low-key, mellow session in which Kate and I talked about what her week had been like. I wondered whether, because of the more optimistic prognosis she had received, she and I were pulling back from the closeness we'd achieved. It felt more like we were living in ordinary time with each other and that the texture of the session was shaped by that and the fact that Kate was a tired patient who had been through a daunting week.

*   *   *

I'm worried. It's past 6:15 p.m., and my appointment with Kate was for 6:00. I wonder where people are when they're late, but I don't usually worry. It's not like she's been having heart problems and could have had a coronary on the way here. There's no emergency tied to cancer. Maybe she fell asleep because she's so tired out from the new chemotherapy.

I called her cell phone and her home and got a recording at each. I'd think maybe the ring or the phone message would have awakened her if she was asleep at home. Screening, Kate usually picks up in the middle of my leaving a message.

I look at the pen and ink drawings on the wall at the foot of my couch, done by my patient Fiona. She gave them to me when she was ending treatment. They hang one over the other. The one on the bottom depicts a man hunched over, crying. There's something about his shoulders—their size, the way they're hunched—that conveys a human being who is very grief stricken. When Fiona first showed it to me, I got tears in my eyes. I used to look at it often when I was sitting idly in my office.

But the last couple of years my eyes have been more drawn to the pen and ink drawing that hangs above the grief-stricken man. It's a drawing of a mother and child, the child cradled in the mother's arms. The mother's arms are big, her hands strong, holding the baby close to her. She is looking off and away, into the distance. I wonder if she is seeing her child's future, perhaps some tragic event.

At 6:40, the phone rang and it was Kate. She is very tired out from this new and more powerful chemotherapy, and she fell asleep some time before our appointment. A moment after Kate called, my next patient rang the buzzer. Kate and I talked a few minutes, and then I asked if she would like me to call her after my next session. She said no, she would talk to me the following Wednesday. I wonder how much my ambivalence came through in my offer. I would have liked to talk with her, and yet, I had had a long day and wanted to go home.

*   *   *

In Ernest Becker's (1973) classic book *The Denial of Death*, Becker maintains that the fear of death is a universal terror from which none of us is immune. We all have an ever-present fear of death. If this fear were constantly conscious we would be unable to function, and so we repress it. The paradox is that, unconsciously, we live with an ever-present fear of death, while, consciously, we live "in utter obliviousness to this fear in our conscious life" (Becker, p. 17).

In the face of death or a life-threatening illness, the unconscious fear begins to emerge into the conscious mind and those affected move into a liminal space, one in which the threshold of repression is crossed. They then live in a transitional space as described by Winnicott (1953). It is a space of being neither here nor there and simultaneously here *and* there, a paradoxical space between realities and, yet, constituting a reality of its own, in which one begins to emotionally grasp the finiteness of being. Frommer (2005) described this time as one in which there is "a powerful shift in subjectivity":

> There is often considerable flux and instability in any mind's struggle with its own mortality. But the struggle can be psychologically liberating.... Being with the transience of existence can enliven the capacity to savor life, order priorities, tolerate losses and limitations (Yalom, 1980), and grant ourselves permission to take chances and make mistakes. Finding the liberating potential of mortality is, at best, an unstable achievement that is not easily won. (p. 482)

* * *

After Kate started her new regimen of chemotherapy last week, she felt awful. Her body ached all over, and she was constantly tired. She didn't know if becoming achy was a side effect of chemotherapy. She had a cough she'd never had before and worried it might be pneumonia.

She saw her radiologist on Friday, who showed her the PET scan. When she asked him, "What about the main tumor?" he responded, "It's gone." She thinks that's what he said. But she has begun to doubt it. "It would just be preposterous," she said. "This was the same tumor that was supposed to kill me within the month. It doesn't feel right that it would be gone. I feel something's wrong," she said.

I knew the doctors had not given Kate much hope, but it wasn't until that day that I found out they'd only given her a month to live. Kate explained that when she was told that, she thought it was "a stupid statement" and "pushed it away."

Kate hated the physical state she was in, not only because she was not feeling well but also because she thought it was "a huge waste of time." She said, "I'm a five by eighter," and explained that at the beginning of every week she wrote down all she had to do that week on a 5″ by 8″ index card. Then each morning she wrote down what she had to do that day on a 4″ by 6″ card, and if she "overreached" and there were items she didn't get to she wrote them down on the next day's 4″ by 6″ card. "It works and I love my cards," she said.

Kate said there was something from our previous session she wanted to return to with me. "When I said to you I'd 'worked the office' at my doctor's, you said, 'Oh, Kate.' Did it bother you that I said that? It sounds manipulative, but I didn't mean it to."

I agreed it did sound manipulative and said what I was reacting to was not that she was manipulative, but that she covered over the vulnerable part of her by saying something flippant rather than saying something about how attached she'd gotten to the office staff and that she would miss them. Kate responded that she should stop saying she "works" people because it's not what she means, even though she says it. She continued, "The people in that office are people who've been with me through the most dangerous, critical part of my life. I'll never forget them."

* * *

Kate called a couple of hours before our weekly appointment and left a message saying she had had a setback and was in the hospital and would call as soon as she was able. I feel afraid for her.

I sit waiting for the phone to ring. The church bells across the street ring six times. It makes me think of death, "for whom the bell tolls." The church bells were striking 10:00 as we processed into the church at my father's funeral. One moment we were all standing around at the funeral home, and the next moment, a prayer said, we were in the limousine on the way to the church.

I check my watch. It's only 2 minutes after 6:00. I fear for Kate's life. Her voice didn't sound good on her message. I wonder what it is that is wrong, what has happened. It seems ominous. She had gotten such good reports from her doctor. As she herself said, "No one used the word miracle, but they stopped just short of that."

I wonder if her esophagus closed up again and she isn't in the hospital because of the cancer, but because she can't swallow again. But that makes no sense. The only reason she couldn't swallow is because of the tumor on her esophagus, which has disappeared with the chemotherapy and radiation.

It's 6:10. I do wish the phone would ring. It's hard to sit here just waiting. I wish I knew what it is that has gone wrong. I check to make sure the ringer is turned on on the phone.

I gaze around my office and listen to the sound of cars I'm seldom aware of below on Broadway. A horn blows. Another horn blows back. A subway passes. The vase on the glass tabletop rattles a bit. The bonsai tree is starting to look a little shaggy. I don't know how one trims it. Its shape was so perfect when my patient Margaret gave it to me at Christmastime. The bulb has burned out in the torchiere lamp. Edges of objects are blunted in shadow.

I know Kate hates the hospital. Being in the hospital makes her angry. I wonder if she is afraid and think, "How could she not be afraid?" How could anyone with cancer not be afraid? Her fear tends to convert quickly into anger and irritability. I know that dynamic myself. It's a mechanism we both tend toward.

She said she'd call as soon as she was able. It's now 6:25. I consider calling her cell phone number, but quickly decide against it. If she were able to talk to me now, she would be calling.

I wonder if her children are at the hospital with her. I imagine her daughter is. She's self-employed so she can set her own schedule, and she is devoted to her mother.

I think about what it would be like to lose my mother. It's not a place I want to go, and I turn away from the thought, looking up at the poster of Un Ballo in Maschera on the wall. A woman with a mask in hand is standing between two men. All of their faces look like masks—lifeless, taut, a hollowness about their gaze.

It was just last Friday Kate called and said her PET scan looked so good. Today is only Wednesday. What could have gone wrong?

The buzzer rings. It is my next patient.

* * *

When Kate hadn't called by the next morning, I decided to give her a call. I expected to leave a message for her on her cell phone and was surprised when she answered. Her voice sounded tight, low, uneven, and raspy. I heard her ask her son to leave the room, saying she'd be about 10 minutes. She began by saying to me, "Don't be too kind to me. When people are kind it makes me cry and I can't stand that." She said she was back in the hospital. She had a hole in her esophagus and her doctors were trying to figure out just what to do about it. She kept coughing while she tried to speak and I asked her why she was coughing so much. She said her saliva was going into her lungs because of the hole in her esophagus. She was unable to eat or drink anything. I asked how she got the hole in her esophagus. She said the doctors weren't sure—maybe from the tumor itself or from the radiation used to remove the tumor. I could hear some commotion in the background. A nurse came into the room to check on Kate's IV. "People just walk in and out of here like nothing is happening," Kate said.

This Friday the doctors will do surgery to insert a feeding tube in Kate. Next Tuesday they will perform surgery on her to insert a stent in her esophagus so that food and liquid will bypass the hole and she can eat and drink. The surgeon who will perform that surgery told Kate they weren't at all certain it would work and that she would probably die.

I couldn't believe that she was saying that she would probably die. Everything had been going so well. She'd just been told last week the PET scan showed that the tumor on her esophagus was gone. It must have been the radiation that did it, I thought. Kate's coughing worsened. She said she had to go, that talking aggravated her coughing. I asked her what she'd like to do about our being in contact. She said she didn't know. I said if it was all right with her, I'd like to call to check in on her. She said that would be fine.

My next hour was free. I went outside. Walking through Washington Square Park, I was struck by my incredulity at Kate saying she thought she would probably die. How could I have thought everything had been going so well? A lot had been going well, but it was going well in the context of Kate having a very serious life-threatening disease from which she'd been told it was likely she would die. My denial seemed to cycle in and out, surprising me when I caught it, and, I'm certain, there were many moments of it I did not recognize.

* * *

The following afternoon I called Kate and she answered. She said she was waiting to be taken down to surgery for the feeding tube. The surgery was supposed to be at 3:00 p.m., and it was already 4:00. She said it was hard waiting. Kate struggled coughing all the while we talked and then said she couldn't talk through the coughing and would call me when she could.

It was late Saturday night when I finished reading the early edition of the Sunday *Times*. I thought of Kate and felt the impulse to reread the last piece of what I'd written about her over the previous couple of days. Somehow, reading what I'd written gave me comfort and helped me feel less shaky about Kate's prognosis. Then I called my office voice mail to see if Kate had called. There was a message from her from 6:11 a.m. on Saturday.

Her voice was still raw and gravelly. She said she wanted me to know she was feeling better emotionally than she had been since she went into the hospital on Tuesday. She was "calmer, not so quick to tears and a lot more positive" than she had been since she went into the hospital on Tuesday. She said she didn't want me to worry, but did want me to know how much my caring meant to her.

* * *

Kate's daughter called and left a message saying her mother was doing well. She'd had the surgery to insert the stent in her esophagus and been in the ICU but was now back on a regular floor. Her mother asked her to call me to let me know what was happening and to tell me she would like to talk to me.

I called back as soon as I got the message and reached Kate's daughter. I heard her tell her mom she would leave the room so Kate could talk to me. Kate's voice was low and flat, and she wasn't coughing anymore. I told her how relieved I was to hear the surgery had gone all right and to hear her voice. She said to me, "I think ..." and something about dying I couldn't quite decipher. I asked her to repeat what she'd said and she responded, "I kind of think I'm going to die." She said they were still trying to work out how to keep the passageways to her lungs and esophagus separated. Her lungs had collapsed while she was in ICU, and they had to perform a terribly painful procedure to inflate her lungs again.

"I don't know," Kate said. "Before I felt safe, that no matter what happened I would be safe. That's gone. I don't feel that anymore. There's a lot of blackness now. It's like there's blackness all around."

I said, "Of course half of you feels like you're going to die. How would you not?"

She thanked me for understanding and said she needed to say she thought she might die and she needed it to be heard, and that's why she had wanted to talk to me. Everyone at the hospital was focusing on all the things that were going right, and there were things going right but not everything. I told her I knew how lonely and isolated it made her feel. I ended by saying, "I'm here for you." She said goodbye through tears.

As I am writing this, the song "Amazing Grace" peals out from the bell tower across the street at Grace Episcopal Church. My sister Mary had suggested we sing it at my father's funeral, and the organist played it at communion. The words go through my mind:

Amazing grace, how sweet the sound
That saved a wretch like me.
I once was lost, but now I'm found
Was blind, but now I see.

I think of what the words are saying. Grace is the difference between lost and found, blind and seeing. When it comes down to it, those states arise as gifts inside of us—part a product of our will and work, and part mystery or blessing.

I recall the recession down the main aisle of the church behind my father's casket. The incense was comforting, as were the words of the recessional hymn—"And I will raise him up, and I will raise him up, I will raise him up on the last day."

I think about going to see Kate in the hospital. I don't even know if I could do it without a car. Then I think there must be cabs at the Tarrytown train station, and I could call to get a cab back to the train. The church bells ring six times. It's Wednesday, my regular appointment time with Kate.

I wonder how she would feel about me coming to the hospital. I suppose that I would talk to her about my coming there ahead of time. I see myself by her bed holding her hand—and screwing up the courage to be with her in the possibility she might be dying. It seems like an awesome task, a work about which I know so little. Maybe she wouldn't want me to come to the hospital. When her daughter was telling me on the phone that Kate looked much better than she had and that her coloring was returning, in the background Kate said, "I look like hell."

How do I hold this reality, the reality that it is possible that Kate will die? How do I help her hold it and offer myself to her as a person with whom she can hold it? I stop writing to call Metro North to get the train schedule.

* * *

Kate didn't want me to come to the hospital. She said she didn't want me to see her the way she looked. We had our regular session a few days later over the phone. Kate was home and very weak, tired and thin, but feeling better than she had in the hospital. In less than 2 weeks she'd undergone major surgery three times and, as she remarked, "had a major trauma" to her emotions.

Kate said, "They said I was fine, and then I woke up and boom, I'm laid out in the hospital. I received Last Rites and the whole thing when my lungs collapsed. It unsettles you. The truth is that every day you wake up, you don't know how that day will end. But we cannot, and never do, look at that constantly, or we wouldn't function. I need that illusion back, or part of it. Anything can happen in a minute. When you run into that fact as quickly as I did, it's not so easy to put the illusion back in place."

REFERENCES

Adams-Silvan, A. (1994). "That darkness—is about to pass": The treatment of a dying patient. *Psychoanalytic Studies of the Child*, 49, 328–348.

Adelman, A. (1995). Traumatic memory and the intergenerational transmission of holocaust narratives. *Psychoanalytic Studies of the Child*, 50, 343–367.

Auerhahn, N. C., & Laub, D. (1984). Annihilation and restoration: Posttraumatic memory as pathway and obstacle to recovery. *International Journal of Psycho-Analysis*, 11, 327–344.

Bass, A. (2001). It takes one to know one: Or, whose unconscious is it anyway? *Psychoanalytic Dialogues*, 11, 683–702.

Becker, E. (1973). *The denial of death*. New York: Free Press.

Bettelheim, B. (1983). *Freud and man's soul*. New York: Random House.

Boulanger, G. (2002a). The cost of survival: Psychoanalysis and adult onset trauma. *Contemporary Psychoanalysis*, 38, 17–44.

Boulanger, G. (2002b). Wounded by reality: The collapse of the self in adult onset trauma. *Contemporary Psychoanalysis*, 38, 45–76.

Davoine, F., & Gaudilliére, J. M. (2004). *History beyond trauma*. New York: Other Press.

Demaris, O. (1969). *Captive city*. New York: Lyle Stuart.

Dupont, J. (1994). Freud's analysis of Ferenczi as revealed by their correspondence. *International Journal of Psycho-Analysis*, 75, 301–320.

Eliot, T. S. (1944). Dry savages. *Four Quartets* (pp. 33–48). New York: Harcourt.

Eliot, T. S. (1963). Ash wednesday. *Selected Poems* (pp. 81–96). New York: Harcourt.

Fanon, F. (1963). *The wretched of the earth*. New York: Grove.

Ferenczi, S. (1929). The principle of relaxation and neocatharsis. In M. Balint (Ed.), *Final contributions to the problems and methods of psycho-analysis* (E. Mosbacher, Trans.; pp. 108–129). London: Karnac.

Ferenczi, S. (1931). Child-analysis in the analysis of adults. In M. Balint (Ed.), *Final Contributions to the problems and methods of psychoanalysis* (E. Mosbacher, Trans.; pp. 126–143). London: Karnac Books.

Ferenczi, S. (1933, September 4). The confusion of tongues. Paper presented at the Twelfth Psychoanalytic Congress, Weisbaden, Germany.

Ferenczi, S. (1988). *The clinical diary of Sándor Ferenczi* (J. Dupont, Ed.; M. Balint & N. S. Jackson, Trans.). Cambridge, MA: Harvard University Press. (Originally published in 1932)

Ferenczi, S., & Rank, O. (1924). *The development of psycho-analysis.* Madison, CT: International Universities Press.

Fresco, N. (1984). Remembering the unknown. *International Journal of Psycho-Analysis, 22,* 417–427.

Freud, S. (1914). Observations on transference love. In *The standard edition of the complete works of Sigmund Freud* (Vol. 12, pp. 157–171). London: Hogarth.

Freud, S. (1933). Entry 1244, April 2, 1933. In E. Falzedar and E. Brabant (Eds.), *The correspondence of Sigmund Freud and Sandor Ferenczi* (P. Hoffer, Trans.; Vol. 3, 1920–1933, pp. 448–449). Cambridge, MA and London: The Belknap Press of Harvard University Press.

Freud, S. (2000). Remembering, repeating and working-through (further recommendations on the technique of psycho-analysis II). In J. Strachey, (Ed.), *The standard edition of the complete works of Sigmund Freud* (Vol. 12, pp. 145–156). New York: Norton. (Originally published in 1921)

Frommer, M. S. (2005). Living in the liminal spaces of mortality. *Psychoanalytic Dialogues, 15*(4), 479–498.

Gentry, C. (1991). *Hoover: The man and the secrets.* New York: Norton.

Guntrip, H. (1968). *Schizoid phenomena, object relations, and the self.* New York: International Universities Press.

Guntrip, H. (1971). *Psychoanalytic theory, therapy, and the self: A basic guide to the human personality in Freud, Erikson, Klein, Sullivan, Fairbairn, Hartmann, Jacobson, and Winnicott.* New York: Basic.

Herman, J. (1992). *Trauma and recovery.* New York: Basic.

Hillman, J. (1996). *The soul's code: In search of character and calling.* New York: Random House.

Hoffman, I. (1979). Death anxiety and adaptation to mortality in psycho-analytic theory. *Annual of Psychoanalysis, 7,* 233–267.

Horney, K. (1937). *The neurotic personality of our time.* New York: Norton.

Klein, M. (1984). *Love, guilt and reparation, and other works.* New York: Free Press.

Knoblauch, S. H. (1995). The selfobject function of religious experience: The treatment of a dying patient. *Progress in Self Psychology, 11,* 107–217.

Leary, K. (1995). Interpreting in the dark: Race and ethnicity in psychoanalytic psychotherapy. *Psychoanalytic Psychology, 12,* 127–140.

Leary, K. (1997a). Race in psychoanalytic space. *Gender and Psychoanalysis, 2,* 157–172.

Leary, K. (1997b). Race, self-disclosure, and "forbidden talk": Race and ethnicity in contemporary clinical practice. *Psychoanalytic Quarterly, 66,* 163–189.

Leary, K. (2000). Racial enactments in dynamic treatment. *Psychoanalytic Dialogues, 10,* 639–653.

Little, M. (1985). Winnicott working in areas where psychotic anxieties predominate. *Free Associations, 9,* 9–42.

Little, M. (1987). On the value of regression to dependence. *Free Associations, 10*, 7–22.

Locker, B. (2007). End of mommy: What happens in psychoanalysis when the analyst's mother dies. Paper presented at the meeting of the International Association of Relational Psychoanalysis and Psychotherapy, Athens, Greece.

Maso, C. (2000). *Break every rule: essays on language, longing, and moments of desire*. Washington, DC: Counterpoint.

Menaker, E. (1982). *Otto Rank: A rediscovered legacy*. New York: Columbia University Press.

Merton, T. (1971). *Contemplative prayer*. Garden City, NY: Image.

Merton, T. (1972). *New seeds of contemplation*. New York: New Directions. (Originally published in 1962)

Merton, T. (1993). *The courage for truth: The letters of Thomas Merton to writers*. New York: Harcourt Brace.

Morrison, T. (1992). *Playing in the dark*. Cambridge, MA: Harvard University Press.

Prince, R. (1985). Knowing the Holocaust. *Psychoanalytic Inquiry, 5*, 51–61.

Rank, O. (1945). *Will therapy and truth and reality*. New York: Knopf. (Originally published in 1936)

Rank, O. (1968). *Art and artist: Creative urges and personality development*. New York: Agathon.

Shabad, P. (2001). To live before dying: Commentary on paper by Anthony Bass. *Psychoanalytic Dialogues, 11*, 703–709.

Sparks, N. (1996). *The notebook*. New York: Warner.

Teresa of Avila. (1960). *The Life of Teresa of Jesus: The autobiography of Teresa of Avila* (E. Allison Peers, Ed. and trans.). New York: Image Books.

Teresa of Avila. (1961). *Interior castle*. Garden City, NY: Image. (Originally published in 1577)

Therese of Lisieux. (1938). *The story of a soul: The autobiography of St. Therese of Lisieux*. Westminster, MD: Newman. (trans. M. Day, originally published in 1899)

Therese of Lisieux. (1958). *The auto-biography of St. Therese of Lisieux* (V. Johnson, Trans.). New York: P.J. Kennedy & Sons. (Originally published in 1899)

Thomas, D. (1938). Do not go gentle into that good night. In *The poems of Dylan Thomas*. New York: New Directions.

Tuttle, W. M., Jr. (1996). *Race riot: Chicago in the Red Summer of 1919*. Urbana: University of Illinois Press.

Ulanov, A. (1996). *The functioning transcendent: A study in analytical psychology*. Wilmette, IL: Chiron.

White, J. C. (2007). Impact of race and ethnicity upon transference and countertransference. Paper presented at the Metropolitan Institute for Training in Psychoanalytic Psychotherapy, New York.

Winnicott, D. W. (1953). Transitional phenomena–A study of the first not-me possession. *International Journal of Psycho-Analysis, 34*, 89–97.

Winnicott, D. W. (1967). The location of cultural experience. *International Journal of Psycho-Analysis, 46*, 372.

Winnicott, D. W. (1974). Fear of breakdown. *International Journal of Psycho-Analysis, 1*, 103–107.

Yalom, I. (1980). *Existential psychotherapy.* New York: Basic.

Index